500 FACTS
History

www.pegasusforkids.com

© B. Jain Publishers (P) Ltd. All rights reserved. No part of this book may be reproduced, stored in a retrieval system or transmitted, in any form or by any means, mechanical, photocopying, recording or otherwise, without any prior written permission of the publisher.

Published by Kuldeep Jain for B. Jain Publishers (P) Ltd., D-157, Sector 63, Noida - 201307, U.P. Registered office: 1921/10, Chuna Mandi, Paharganj, New Delhi-110055

Printed in India

CONTENTS

Preface 5

INTRODUCTION

Prehistoric Evolution 6

The First of the Human Race 16

The Formation of Civilisations 26

Livelihood Develops 40

EMPIRES

The Creation of Empires 52

NEW WORLD

The Beginning (CE 1-400) 64

RELIGIOUS HISTORY

Religious World (400-800 CE) 75

Medieval Period 86

ART AND CULTURE

History of Art and Culture 96

EMPERORS, KINGS AND LEADERS

Famous Rulers 106

NEW LANDS

The Explorers 116

CHANGING WORLD

The Industrial Revolution 126
Histories of the Continents 136
The World Wars 152

EXPANDING WORLD

A Global Outreach 168
Important Personalities 176
The World Today 186

PREFACE

Why do we need history? We often wonder about this, don't we?

Well, history is important because it tells us about how far humankind has come, from being great apes that roamed aimlessly to devising objects that give us information at our fingertips. It is important because we learn of the mistakes humankind has made in the hope that we never repeat them.

500 Facts on History traces this journey of humankind in a fast-facts format. This book aims to take you back in time when Earth was formed and helps you travel through various events that have defined not just our past, but have shaped our present.

We not only aim to enhance your understanding of the history of the world, but also hope that these facts will help add value to your knowledge of many things around you.

Happy Reading, Kids!

INTRODUCTION

Prehistoric Evolution

1 Scientists studying the Earth have found proof that there have been phases when the Earth's overall temperatures were much lower than they are today. Most parts of our planet was covered under snow and ice. As the ice from this era melted it gave birth to new oceans. It was around this time when Pangaea broke up and drifted apart. Did you know that the Himalayas were formed when the piece of land that is now India collided with the larger landmass of Asia?

PREHISTORIC EVOLUTION

2 Scientists believe that millions of years ago there was a cosmic explosion called the Big Bang. This led to the formation of the universe and all its constituents. It gave birth to the stars and the planets. The Earth was created 4600 million years ago and life on the planet began 570 million years ago.

3 **Today, the world is divided into seven continents, but it was not always like this.** Before the land split and took on the present shape, it was one big supercontinent called Pangaea. Slowly the continents broke away from the supercontinent and came to the position that they are in today.

4 **The word prehistoric means 'before history'.** The word is made up of two words—the Latin 'pr' and the Greek 'historia'. Numerous plants and animals came into being on Earth much before human beings developed as a species. In fact, many of the animals and other life forms became extinct even before the first humans on this planet learned to talk!

INTRODUCTION

5 It is hard to believe, but more than 99.9 per cent of all living creatures that have ever lived on this planet are already extinct! One of the biggest mass extinctions was the Permian-Triassic extinction, which took place around 250 million years ago. It is a fact that new species replace old ones. Thus, dinosaurs appeared after the Permian-Triassic extinction.

6 You would be surprised to know that animals (as we know them today) were not the first life forms present on Earth. The first inhabitants of Earth were simple life forms like bacteria and algae! They appeared some 3500 million years ago on the planet. It was only around 570 million years ago that other complex creatures developed.

7 The first complex creatures to make their appearance were jawless fish and invertebrates. Slowly, creatures like the jawed fish came into being. Over time, life moved from the sea onto land, and gradually, amphibians transformed into reptiles.

PREHISTORIC EVOLUTION

8 **Life on land began when plants started to take root near the water bodies.** As a result, animals which fed on plants started living on land. In turn, they provided food for carnivorous animals who began to thrive on land as well.

9 **The Mesozoic era is also called the Age of Reptiles.** This period is dated from about 252 million years ago to 66 million years ago. It came after the great extinction, when new species of plant and animal life were slowly growing on Earth. Mammals came into being and a new array of life forms started dominating the planet. During this period, dinosaurs evolved and populated the Earth.

10 **Around 65 million years ago, dinosaurs faced a huge mass extinction.** The cause of their extinction is still a mystery. However, volcanic eruption and meteorite crashes are suspected to be some of the possible reasons. It was after they had died out that more and more mammals developed and thrived.

INTRODUCTION

11 The two-horned Triceratops is believed to have been one of the last surviving dinosaurs. These were heavy creatures that ate plants to sustain themselves. They had a frill-like structure around the neck which acted as a means of defence against attacks. They also had claws which were hoof-like in appearance.

12 Fossils of spiders have been found from as far back as 360-290 million years ago. This means that they were probably among the first insects to roam on the Earth. Interestingly, spiders have not shown any drastic changes in their form over millions of years.

Tyrannosaurus is one of the best known dinosaurs.

PREHISTORIC EVOLUTION

13 The ancestors of modern birds can be traced back to the age of dinosaurs. The Archaeopteryx is the earliest known bird-like creature. It lived approximately 150 million years ago. It had features like a reptile but had clear feather markings. It could not fly very well. If an Archaeopteryx and a modern bird were to compete in a flying competition, the Archaeopteryx would lose!

14 Have you heard about the dinosaur Tyrannosaurus Rex? It was the largest carnivorous animal who hunted on land. It stood on its rear legs and had small front hands. Based on the fossils that have been found, it stood almost 40 feet long and 13 feet tall.

INTRODUCTION

15 **The ancestor of the modern day horses and other similar animals was the Hyracotherium.** It thrived in the present day North America and Europe some 55 million years ago. It was an herbivore who lived in forests. It was quite small in size, rising only 12 inches in height.

16 **Hominids are the most recent ancestors of humans.** Some scientists consider humans to be the only hominids, but more and more experts include all the great apes into this category. Thus, this would include humans, orangutans and chimpanzees!

17 **Mammals dominated the Earth after dinosaurs became extinct.** Mammals like bats, dolphins, and other animals that we know today came into being at this time. Most importantly, this is when the first primates appeared. They were the ancestors of present day apes and monkeys.

Mammals came into their own after the extinction of dinosaurs.

PREHISTORIC EVOLUTION

18 An early ancestor of humans and apes was the Proconsul, a primitive ape which lived approximately 20 million years ago. However, scientists have identified that Homo sapiens probably evolved from the Australopithecus, whose remains have been found in East Africa. Australopithecus literally means 'Southern Ape'. These seem to have been the first primates to stand on two feet.

19 About 32 million years ago, the first primates who could grasp things with their hands evolved on Earth. Humans, apes, and monkeys are all primates who have evolved differently.

20 A female Australopithecus fossil was discovered in 1974 in Ethiopia. It came to be popularly known as 'Lucy' because, at the time of the discovery, the song 'Lucy in the sky with diamonds' by The Beatles was playing at the excavation camp. Lucy walked on two feet, and was just 1.1 metres (3.7 feet) tall.

INTRODUCTION

21 The most definite evidence that the Australopithecines could walk on two legs was found in 1978 in Laetoli, Tanzania, in East Africa. A set of footprints were discovered here, imprinted in the rock. Scientists believe that a volcano must have erupted in that area about 3.6 million years ago. When the lava started to cool, the Australopithecine must have walked over it, preserving the footsteps.

22 **Homo habilis was an early hominid.** The term literally means 'handy man'. It was given this name because some ancient tools were found with the first fossils of this kind when they were discovered. They had a larger brain size as compared to Australopithecus.

23 **One of the most famous fossil grounds is Olduvai Gorge, in Tanzania.** It seems to have been a prehistoric lake, near which hominids lived. Fossil remains of Homo habilis, Homo erectus and Australopithecus were found there along with many old stone tools.

PREHISTORIC EVOLUTION

24 **The first hominids that truly resembled the modern day man were the Neanderthals.** They were of a smaller build than Homo sapiens. They made clothes out of animal skins and other materials. They also used many different weapons and tools. Interestingly, their skull sizes seem to have been larger than those of modern humans, indicating larger brains.

25 **The first hominids to leave Africa are believed to have been the Homo erectus.** They first moved to Asia and then to Europe. They made new types of tools from stones to hunt. They also seem to have discovered fire, and lived and moved about in groups.

The First of the Human Race

26 **Neanderthals became extinct approximately 30,000 years ago.** The only species of the hominid family 'Homo' that have survived till today are the Homo sapiens sapiens, that is, the present day humans.

27 **The first remains of the Neanderthal man was found in the Neander valley in Germany** ('tal' is the German word for 'valley'). Remains were later found in many other parts of Europe as well. They were hunters, and hunted huge animals, like the woolly mammoth, in large groups. They seem to have lived in caves. The Neanderthal man became extinct about 40,000 years ago.

THE FIRST OF THE HUMAN RACE

28 Homo sapiens sapiens moved out of the cave dwellings of their ancestors, and built homes of their own. It is believed that the basic structure of their houses must have been made from wooden posts and then covered with animal skins or mud. Can you compare that with our modern houses?

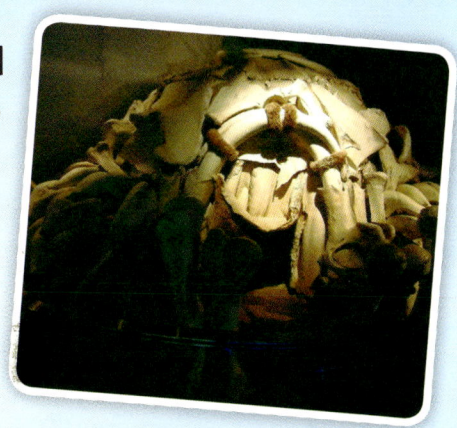

29 Homo sapiens sapiens reached Australia by 40,000 BCE. It is believed that the first settlers used fishing as their main occupation. However, they gradually moved and settled inland. This was both out of a desire to explore and need for new food resources.

Neanderthals depended heavily on hunting to fulfill their food requirements.

30 The first counting devices were found in the Border Cave in South Africa. Here, archaeologists discovered wooden sticks and baboon bones with parallel lines carved on them. It is believed that they were used as tools for counting.

INTRODUCTION

31 The word 'aboriginals' means 'inhabitants from earliest times'. The early humans improved the tool technology that had been used by the hominids for thousands of years. They learned to sharpen the flint stone and attached it to sticks to make axes by 30,000 BCE. They used the tools to cut down forests in order to create more space for settlements.

32 Early humans used the cave or rocks as a canvas for art. They drew pictures of animals and humans. They drew scenes of hunting, as well as scenes that show groups of people living together. They often drew commonly seen animals of the time. These cave paintings have been found all over the world—in Asia, Australia, Africa, and Europe.

33 To make paint to draw, the early humans used different minerals and powdered them before mixing them with water. For example, charcoal (black), hematite (red), chalk (white), and so on were used as these were easily available to them.

THE FIRST OF THE HUMAN RACE

34 **One of the most famous cave paintings in the world were discovered not by archaeologists but by schoolboys!** These are the Lascaux caves in Europe. They date back to the Palaeolithic period, about 15,000-10,000 BCE. They have paintings of animals, such as cows, deer, and bulls. These paintings are very well preserved.

35 **The oldest samples of mobile art, which could be carried around, were found in the Apollo 11 Caves in Namibia.** It was named by German archaeologist W.E. Wendt, who was working on the site when he heard that the spacecraft Apollo 11 had safely returned to Earth. These caves have paintings on the walls, as well as on quartzite stone slabs.

The last ice age is known as the last glacial period.

36 **When the last ice age began around 13,000 BCE, the water level fell and continents were connected by ice sheets.** This made it easier for the early humans to move from one continent to another. It is believed that this was the time when humans moved from Asia over to North America and Alaska, over the frozen Bering Strait.

INTRODUCTION

37 **During the last ice age, the animals hunted by early humans were very different from those we see today.** There were deer-like animals as big as horses, called 'megaceros'. They also hunted mammoths, huge boars and bulls. We know this from the remains of animal bones as well as from the cave paintings.

38 **You may have heard that man is a social animal.** This was definitely true for the early humans. They lived in large groups. This made it easier for them to hunt large animals, and also offered better protection from enemies. They would gather around the animal and then attack it with sharp spears.

39 **Around 13,000 BCE, the Homo sapiens had started gathering and hunting food.** They hunted animals based on where they lived. They made better weapons by sharpening stones of different shapes and sizes, which made hunting easier. Some archaeologists believe that woolly mammoths became extinct because of over-hunting.

Homo sapiens are the only species of human still around today.

THE FIRST OF THE HUMAN RACE

40

Prehistoric times are defined on the basis of the tools used by early humans. Thus, they are known as the Palaeolithic or early stone age, Mesolithic or middle stone age, and Neolithic or new stone age. At each stage, the kind of stone tools and weapons used became more refined according to the kind of work it was used for. Do you know that the hunters in 13,000 BCE used the same kind of hand axe that was created by the Homo erectus some two million years ago? It was a useful tool which was used for cutting wood as well as for cutting through animal flesh and skin.

INTRODUCTION

41 **There seems to have been division of labour among the early humans.** Men were responsible for hunting big prey, while the women and children of the clan were gatherers. They roamed the forest and collected edible berries and nuts. They used instruments like sticks to dig and prod the Earth. They also gathered honey and other food stuff.

42 **It was in the Neolithic period around 10,000 BCE that people first started to sow crops and domesticate animals.** The weather conditions had changed by this time, becoming warmer. The huge animals and heavy foliage of the previous era had started dying out, and instead, smaller creatures like sheep and deer had evolved.

43 **The early humans gradually started domesticating wild animals and breeding them in captivity.** It is believed that they started by keeping animals for food. The first domesticated sheep are traced back to Iraq, around 8700 BCE. However, even before that, dogs had already been domesticated in Eurasia.

THE FIRST OF THE HUMAN RACE

44 **We all know that early humans created fire by striking stones.** They used a special stone to light the fire. Iron pyrites were used and stuck with flints to create sparks. The pyrite stones contain sulphur, which makes it easy for sparks to emerge.

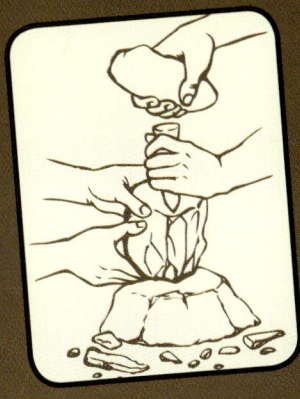

45 **The first evidence of farming comes from Abu Hureyra in Syria.** Grains of rye have been found here from about 11,000 BCE. However, evidence of more organised farming comes from the Middle East, around 9000 BCE. Wheat was one of the first grains to be used in this way by humans.

46 **Early settlements are often found near the river banks.** This gave the settlers easy access to water for their daily use and for farming. After agriculture began, the early farmers started exchanging their excess grain with their neighbours. In return, they would get tools, animals, or other objects. This gave rise to the barter system since there was no money in use at the time.

INTRODUCTION

47 Around 7000 BCE, people started creating stronger, more permanent shelters. They built houses from stone and sometimes used sun-baked bricks made from mud. One of the first such towns was Catal Huyuk in Turkey. Now that the people had an assured food supply through agriculture, they were able to settle in one place for a longer period. The population grew and small settlements grew into villages, and then towns.

48 In the town of Catal Huyuk, the inhabitants seem to have worshipped mysterious gods. Archaeologists have discovered decorated rooms, where the bones of dead family members were kept. A statue was also discovered, which is believed to represent the mother goddess for fertility.

THE FIRST OF THE HUMAN RACE

49 The earliest civilisations are believed to have grown near river valleys. These were the Indus Valley civilisation along the River Indus, the Xia and Shang civilisation along the Yellow River, the Egyptian civilisation along the Nile, and the Mesopotamian or Sumerian civilisation along the banks of the Tigris and Euphrates Rivers.

50 It is believed that these early civilisations had trade relations. Artefacts and seals from the Indus Valley civilisation have been found in Mesopotamia. Similarly, the Egyptian civilisation borrowed certain practices, like writing, from the Sumerians. The Sumerian script was called 'cuneiform'.

51 In Egypt, North Africa, around 5000 BCE, a major civilisation was born. This civilisation flourished on the banks of the River Nile. It was well known for the grandeur of its tombs, its complex social system, and beautiful works of art. The Egyptian civilisation was a 'Bronze Age' civilisation, as humans had discovered and started using metals, especially bronze, at the time.

The Formation of Civilisations

52 **The Egyptian civilisation had its own unique script.** It was very different from the one we use today. The script used pictures rather than alphabets. The Egyptians used these picture characters to form words and used additional symbols to make it comprehensible. This pictographic script was known as 'hieroglyphics'.

53 **The kingdoms of Upper Egypt and Lower Egypt came together as one under the rule of the Pharaoh Menes after many centuries in 3100 BCE.** The Pharaoh made Memphis the capital of the dynasty.

THE FORMATION OF CIVILISATIONS

54 Over time, people from Asia came and settled in the Nile delta. They were known as Hyksos. They had invaded Egypt and took power around 1650 BCE, until they were ultimately defeated by Pharaoh Ahmose I around 1550 BCE.

55 Did you know that the Egyptians mummified several cats too? Cats were considered magical creatures, and were often associated with the cat goddess, Bastet.

Only rich Egyptian could afford the expensive process of mummification.

56 Egyptians mummified their dead because they believed in an afterlife. Before 2300 BCE only Pharaohs were mummified, but after that anyone who could afford it could practice the ritual.

INTRODUCTION

57 **The Pharaohs of Egypt were buried with their treasures after their deaths.** This included not only large amounts of gold and silver, but also food, drinks and even slaves to serve them in the afterlife! One such Pharaoh was Tutankhamun, whose tomb was discovered in 1922. This was one of the richest tombs and several beautiful ancient artefacts were recovered along with a golden throne.

58 **Religion was an important part of life in Mesopotamia.** All the cities had huge temple complexes around which the city was organised. The priests were very powerful. The temples owned land, organised work and conducted trade.

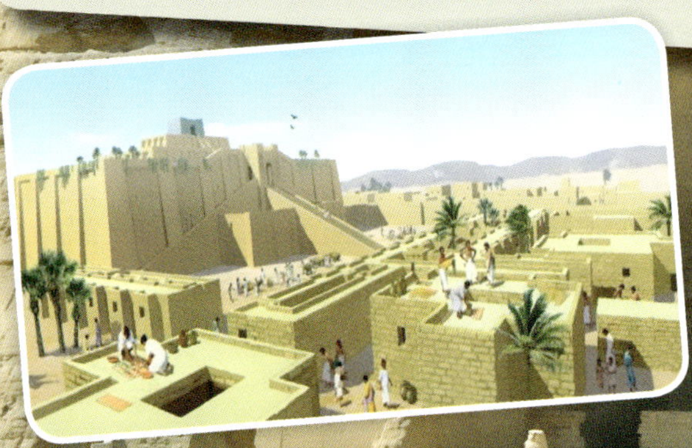

THE FORMATION OF CIVILISATIONS

59 **The area between the Tigris and Euphrates Rivers was the birthplace of the Mesopotamian or Sumerian civilisation.** Mesopotamia means 'land between the rivers'. This area is also known as the cradle of civilisation. Though settlements had existed even earlier, a large scale civilisation with an organised rule, money economy, monumental architecture, cities and regular trade developed sometime around 5000 BCE. Some of the important cities of this civilisation were Ur, Babylon and Nineveh.

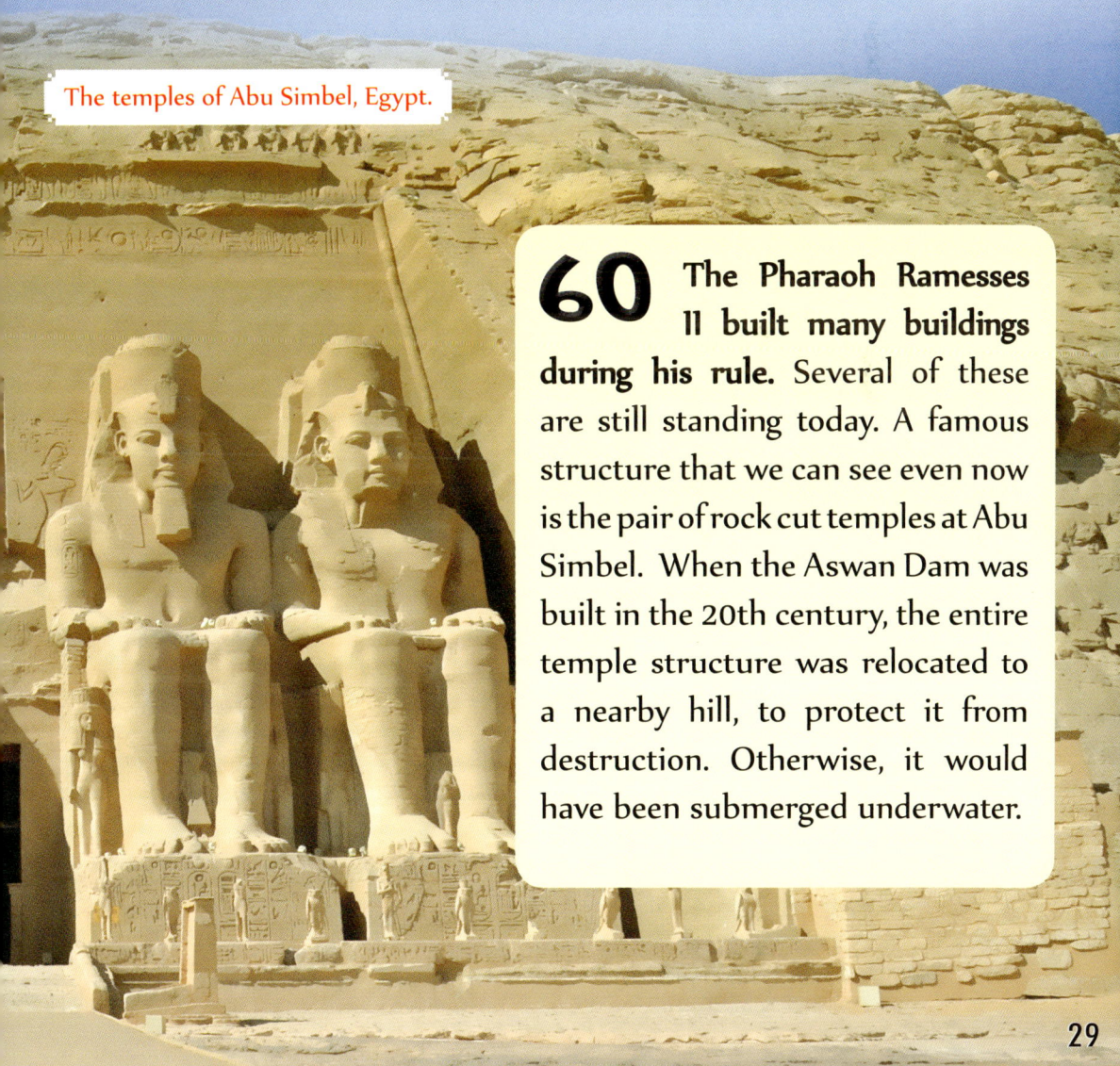

The temples of Abu Simbel, Egypt.

60 **The Pharaoh Ramesses II built many buildings during his rule.** Several of these are still standing today. A famous structure that we can see even now is the pair of rock cut temples at Abu Simbel. When the Aswan Dam was built in the 20th century, the entire temple structure was relocated to a nearby hill, to protect it from destruction. Otherwise, it would have been submerged underwater.

INTRODUCTION

61 Sargon, the king of Akkad, was responsible for uniting the nations of Mesopotamia. He led the establishment of the first major empire, the Akkadian empire. It is believed that everyone feared his army and that he had 5,400 soldiers who ate with him every day!

62 Writing is supposed to be a sign of civilisation. The script was invented by the Sumerians around 3500 BCE. They used pens made out of reed to carve symbols onto clay boards. This cuneiform script was read from left to right.

The archaeological site of Harappa city in Pakistan.

THE FORMATION OF CIVILISATIONS

63 **Hammurabi is considered to be the strongest Babylonian king.** He conquered Sumer and Akkad to bring them together under his rule. Babylon was the capital of his empire. He also introduced many laws and reforms. Did you know that his law code is the longest surviving code in history?

64 **The Indus Valley Civilisation reached its peak around 2500 BCE.** Earlier settlements have been found towards the north, but it is believed that the people moved to the fertile valley of the Indus for better agricultural opportunities. Some of the cities that have been found are Harappa, Mohenjo-daro, and Lothal. These cities were very well planned, along a north-south grid pattern, with wide roads that intersected at right angles. Various structures have been excavated, including a bath house, granary and dockyard.

INTRODUCTION

65 **Mohenjo-daro has an excellent example of a planned drainage system.** The drains ran under the streets and were connected with washrooms in each house on the streets. They had sewage disposal areas located outside the town.

66 **The Indus cities declined after 1,000 years of continuous habitation.** The population seems to have been completely wiped out suddenly. It is suggested that the area may have experienced floods or earthquakes. Some historians also suggest that the remaining population may have been killed by invaders from the north-west.

THE FORMATION OF CIVILISATIONS

67 **The Hittite empire was the first to use iron on a large scale, around 1500 BCE.** They kept the techniques of moulding iron a secret which only came into popular knowledge several centuries later!

68 **Hittites were considered strong because of their well equipped armies.** They used horse chariots which earned them extra leverage over their enemies.

69 **Proof of settlements from the Neolithic period were found in China too.** However, its first major ruling dynasty was the Xia dynasty around 2200 BCE. This civilisation grew around the Yellow River.

Western Xia tombs at the foot of Helan Mountains in Ningxia, China.

INTRODUCTION

70 The Shang dynasty of China took root around 1600 BCE and came to its full power by 1500 BCE. They manufactured textiles made of silk and also developed a complicated writing system. The emperors were buried in royal tombs, along with treasure and the remains of animals and human sacrifices. It is believed that they were buried to keep the king company and serve him even after death.

71 The Shang People used animal bones to predict the future. They sometimes carved questions and their answers onto the bones. These specimens are considered to be earliest records of Chinese script known to humankind.

THE FORMATION OF CIVILISATIONS

72 The Hebrews migrated to Canaan around 1300 BCE. It is believed that Moses, who was a Hebrew leader, led his people through the Sinai desert from Egypt to Canaan. This journey is known as the Exodus in the Bible.

73 The city of Troy was built and destroyed nine times! Homer, the Greek poet, described in his poetic work *The Iliad* how the Greeks used a large wooden horse to invade Troy and defeat it.

INTRODUCTION

74 **Have you ever noticed that companies today have trademarks?** In earlier times the traders of the Mediterranean and Indus Valleys had their own seals which they put on their goods. Like today, people preferred to buy things from popular traders and could identify the products through the seals.

The Newgrange Stone Age Passage Tomb in Newgrange, Ireland.

75

The Phoenicians of Tyre traded what was considered luxury goods, like ivory items, glassware, silver and gold ornaments. At that time, the colour purple was associated with royalty because purple dye was expensive.

76 **Some of the most amazing constructions of the Neolithic in Europe are the tombs marked by huge stones.** A stone tomb was found at Newgrange in Ireland which is believed to date back to around 3200 BCE. It was a passage grave, a common structure in Europe at the time.

THE FORMATION OF CIVILISATIONS

77 **There is a strange megalithic structure in Carnac in France.** It is a dense collection of huge stones or megaliths, arranged in rows or circles. It is believed to date back to about 2400 BCE. Archaeologists believe that they were possibly used to observe stars. These stone structures may also have even been used for public gatherings during ceremonies, rituals and feasts.

78 **People in the earlier ages had many different funeral practices and rites.** By the Bronze Age in Europe, people were often buried together in graves. In England, these graves were formed into mounds or barrows. West Kennet Long Barrow is a good example of such graves.

INTRODUCTION

79 **The Minoan Civilisation developed in the southern Greek island of Crete during the Bronze Age.** The civilisation was named after the legendary King Minos of Crete. This is supposed to have been a very rich kingdom, thanks to its trade across the Mediterranean. The Palace of Knossos, which dates back to this period, stands even today.

80 **There is a Greek folktale about a monster called the Minotaur.** It was believed to be a half-man and half-bull. It lived in the Labyrinth, a complicated maze that King Minos had gotten made. The Minotaur is said to have been defeated by Theseus, a prince of Athens.

THE FORMATION OF CIVILISATIONS

81 In the Arctic region, an evolved form of human civilisation began around 2000 BCE. The subcultures of these people are called Inuit. 'Eskimo' is the term given to them by the Europeans. The harsh weather conditions of the Arctic created a different lifestyle for the Inuit people than those seen in other parts of the world.

82 The people in the Arctic used boats which were covered in animal skin to wade through the cold waters. The closed forms of these boats were called kayaks.

The Inuit, who live in the Arctic, are said to be descended from whale hunters.

Livelihood Develops

83 The Iron Age is considered to have started around 1200 BCE. It is named so because from this time, tools and implements started being made mostly from iron. The Iron Age came after the Bronze Age, where bronze was used to make tools. Before the Bronze Age was the Stone Age, where stone was the dominant material to make tools.

84 In the Korean region, iron technology was introduced in the first millennium BCE. It appears that the technology was introduced into Korea from the northern regions of the continental mainland. Iron was used to produce useful and effective utensils as well as ritual tools and weaponry.

Al Mina archaeological site in Tyre, Lebanon.

85 The Khoisan-speaking people of Africa lived around the Kalahari Desert for many years. These people were hunters by profession and did not grow crops. The Khoisan-speaking people were mostly absorbed by the Bantu-speaking people over time. However, some people managed to maintain their identity and still live in the area today.

LIVELIHOOD DEVELOPS

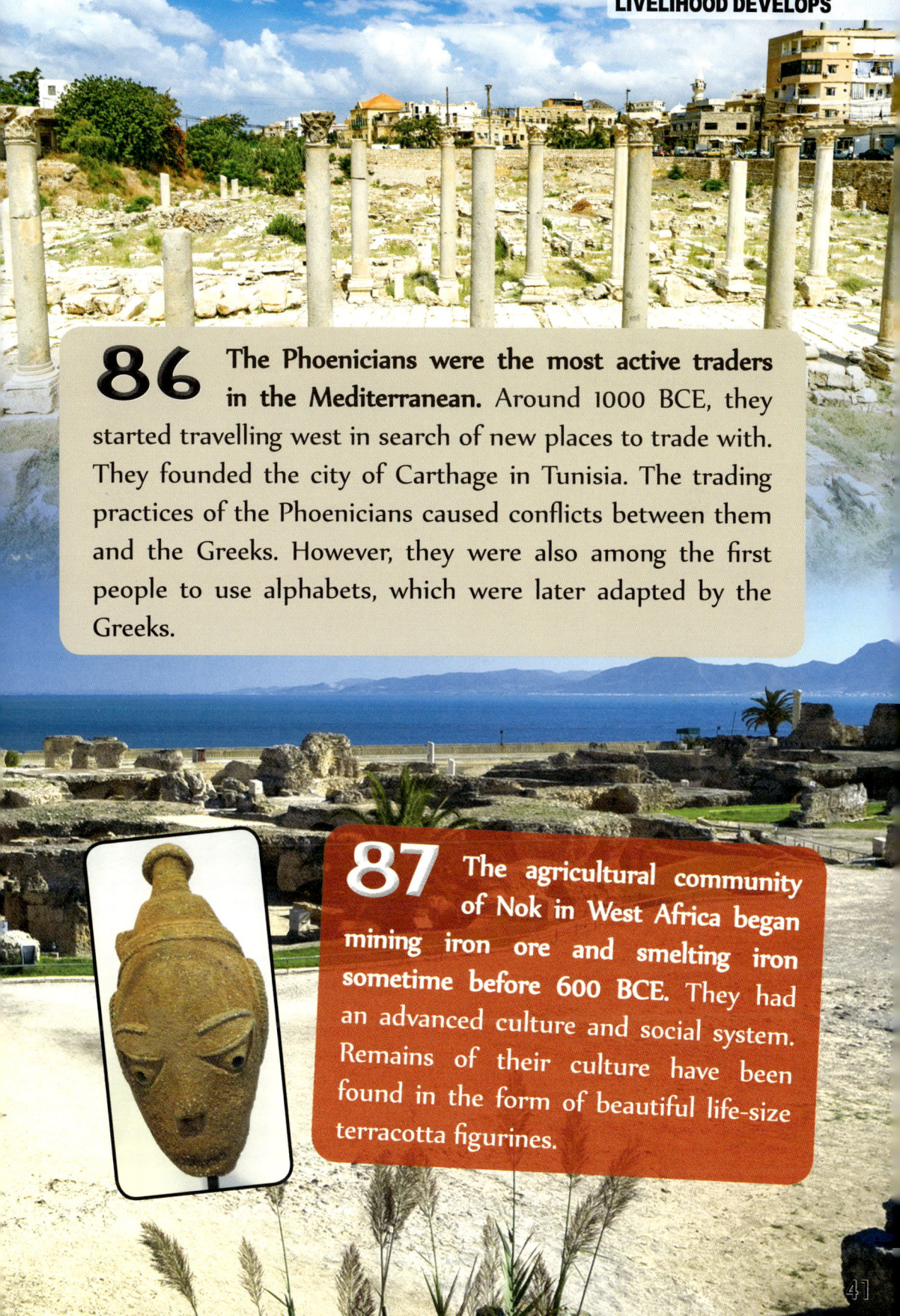

86 **The Phoenicians were the most active traders in the Mediterranean.** Around 1000 BCE, they started travelling west in search of new places to trade with. They founded the city of Carthage in Tunisia. The trading practices of the Phoenicians caused conflicts between them and the Greeks. However, they were also among the first people to use alphabets, which were later adapted by the Greeks.

87 **The agricultural community of Nok in West Africa began mining iron ore and smelting iron sometime before 600 BCE.** They had an advanced culture and social system. Remains of their culture have been found in the form of beautiful life-size terracotta figurines.

INTRODUCTION

88 The Zhou dynasty in China came to power around 1045 BCE. This was a period when the rulers declared they had divine right to rule, or the 'mandate of heaven'. The Zhou people had many skilled artists who worked well with metals like silver. The Zhou dynasty reign is also considered to mark the high point of bronze-ware in China.

89 The Aryans were nomads belonging to central Asia, who moved southwards into Northern India around 1500 BCE. They were aware of iron technology, and when they reached the fertile plains of India, they settled down and took up agriculture. The earliest records found about them are in the form of the four sacred books known as the Vedas.

90 Aryan society had four classes or segregations, based on work. For example, the highest strata were priests (brahmins), the second were the warriors (kshatriyas), the third were the merchant class (vaishyas) and the fourth were the farmers and workers (shudras), who served the upper classes. Initially, this was not a hereditary system. Thus, the child of a shudra could become a kshatriya, and so on.

LIVELIHOOD DEVELOPS

91 The Assyrian kingdom of Mesopotamia began expansion as early as the tenth century BCE. Due to the army's continuous expeditions, the empire expanded. Archaeologists have found remains of their cities and palaces, as well as tablets on which they recorded their accomplishments.

92 The longest culture in the history of early Japan was the Jomon period. It began about 9000 BCE and lasted till 300 BCE. The people of this period were initially hunters and gatherers, but over time they learned how to cultivate crops. They lived in clusters of small huts.

INTRODUCTION

93 **From the Jomon period, archaeologists have found pottery, tools and jewellery made of shell, stone and bone.** Beautifully crafted terracotta earrings have also been found, dating back to about 500 BCE. Some lacquered earthenware and wooden wares have also been discovered, dating back to around 700 BCE.

Assyrian relief of the Royal lion hunt of King Ashurbanipal seen at the British Museum in London, England.

94 **Ashurbanipal was the last great Assyrian king. He was a patron of art who oversaw the construction of many structures.** His capital was the city of Nineveh, where he collected a large number of cuneiform documents. This collection of ancient documents is now known as 'the Library of Ashurbanipal', and is preserved in the British Museum in London.

LIVELIHOOD DEVELOPS

95 The Assyrian temples were huge structures made from baked bricks. They were called 'ziggurats', which meant 'mountain top'. The Mesopotamians considered temples to be a link between Earth and heaven.

96 The 'Babylonian Captivity' or 'Babylonian Exile' is an event that took place around 598-587 BCE. At that time, the Babylonian King Nebuchadnezzar II had captured the Jewish land of Judea. The Jews were forced to live in exile in Babylon until the Persian ruler Cyrus the great captured Babylon and allowed Jews to return to their homeland.

97 A bronze statue of a stag from 750-650 BCE was found in Kish, Babylonia. It is one of the few sculptures that are believed to have survived from that period, and shows the high level of skill that the artisans had achieved in metal work.

INTRODUCTION

98 One of the first areas to produce true metal coins was the wealthy kingdom of Lydia, in present day Turkey. These coins were first produced around the seventh century BCE, and made of an alloy of gold and silver. They were marked with the image of a lion.

99 In Mesopotamia, coins were not used until about 250 BCE. However, precious metals and other methods of exchange had been in use as far back as 2300 BCE. Terms like 'minas' and 'shekels' were used for silver, signifying the weight of the metal as its value. This silver was often in the form of rings or coils, from which the required amount could be weighed.

100 Siddhartha Gautama was a member of a noble household in North India. By this period, city-states had been established and wealth was being accumulated by the ruling classes. However, Gautama gave up his life of luxury and became an ascetic. He spent many years meditating, and finally attained enlightenment.

LIVELIHOOD DEVELOPS

101 After receiving enlightenment in about 528 BCE, Siddhartha Gautama dedicated his life to teaching and spreading his ideas to the people. He came to be known as the Buddha. His followers are known as Buddhists.

102 The city-state civilisation of the Etruscan people was developed in the eight century BCE in Italy. They had an advanced culture and strong trade ties with the Greeks in the south and the Celtics in the north. They later had a heavy influence on Rome and its civilisation.

INTRODUCTION

103
Several examples of Etruscan art have survived, such as terracotta sculptures, metal objects, especially in bronze, and wall paintings. Interestingly, most of the art that we have found from this period, including wall paintings, has been preserved inside tombs.

104
The foundation of Rome is believed to have been laid in 753 BCE on the banks of the Tiber River. In 509 BCE, the Romans adopted a republic system, instead of being ruled by kings.

Tiber River is named after Tiberinus, a king of Alba Longa who drowned in it.

LIVELIHOOD DEVELOPS

105 **According to a legend, Rome was named after its founder Romulus.** He and his brother were abandoned as children and survived after being cared for by a she-wolf. When they grew up, Romulus founded the city of Rome. However, according to archaeological records, the site of Rome had already been settled for many centuries before the traditional date of 753 BCE.

106 **Greece was divided into many city-states with the largest of them being Sparta.** Athens was the commercial capital. The Greek city-states frequently fought amongst themselves, and united only to ward off the danger posed by the Persian Empire.

107 **Athens embraced democracy around the year 590 BCE.** A lord named Solon initiated the reform by which all citizens were given the right to vote on important decisions. However, it is interesting to note that 'citizens' included only rich men who owned a certain amount of property. Women and the poorer classes were not recognised as citizens at all!

INTRODUCTION

108 **The Greeks were great philosophers and thinkers.** Many of the works by great thinkers, such as Socrates, Aristotle, Pythagoras and others, are read even today. Their ideas are the foundation of western thought. The great fresco by the famous artist Raphael depicts two great thinkers, Plato and Aristotle.

109 **The ancient Greeks showed a very advanced cultural identity.** They had well developed myths and legends. They also were excellent artisans, producing many different kinds of painted and glazed pottery. Some of the pottery pieces depict stories from the Greek myths and legends, such as the stories of Hercules, or the legends of the Gods.

110 **Some of the most beautiful buildings in ancient Greece were the temples.** The ancient Greeks were a religious community and strongly believed that their gods took an active interest in human affairs. They believed that the gods lived on top of Mount Olympus.

LIVELIHOOD DEVELOPS

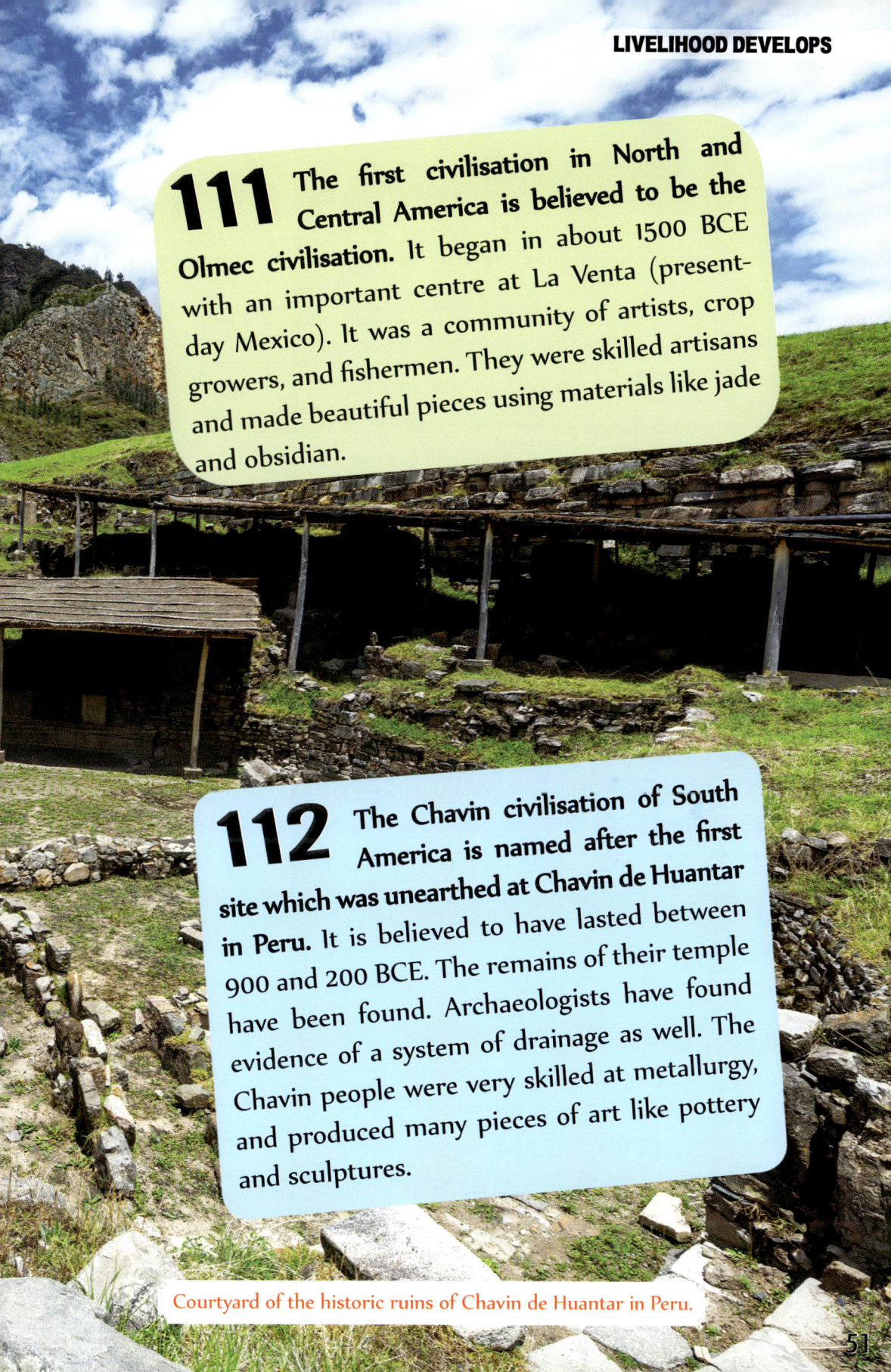

111 **The first civilisation in North and Central America is believed to be the Olmec civilisation.** It began in about 1500 BCE with an important centre at La Venta (present-day Mexico). It was a community of artists, crop growers, and fishermen. They were skilled artisans and made beautiful pieces using materials like jade and obsidian.

112 **The Chavin civilisation of South America is named after the first site which was unearthed at Chavin de Huantar in Peru.** It is believed to have lasted between 900 and 200 BCE. The remains of their temple have been found. Archaeologists have found evidence of a system of drainage as well. The Chavin people were very skilled at metallurgy, and produced many pieces of art like pottery and sculptures.

Courtyard of the historic ruins of Chavin de Huantar in Peru.

EMPIRES

The Creation of Empires

113 When one state or nation rules over another nation or state, it is called an empire. The ruling state is always stronger than the others. Empires are made of a few nations that are ruled by a single emperor or government. One of the first empires was established as early as 3000 BCE when King Narmer of Egypt annexed the surrounding areas and founded the Old Kingdom of Egypt.

114 Empires are formed as a nation grows strong and powerful. It then begins to spread its rule over surrounding areas. The more it spreads, the more powerful it becomes and the more it wants to expand its territory. Eventually empires collapse because it becomes difficult to control such large areas. In the end, they break up into smaller states. For instance, Bronze Age Mesopotamia was ruled by the Akkadian, Babylonian and Assyrian empires before being defeated by the Achaemenid empire.

115 At the beginning of 500 BCE, the strongest and largest empire was the Achaemenid or Persian Empire. It was founded by Cyrus the Great of the Achaemenian dynasty. It was the largest of the ancient empires and stretched from the western Balkans to the northern Caucasus Mountains, the eastern Indus Valley and the southern Persian Gulf.

THE CREATION OF EMPIRES

116 **The Persian Empire was stronger and different from the other empires in the past because of its excellent administration.** The Persians developed a centralised system of administration where the entire empire was divided into different provinces. Each province was ruled by a satrap who reported to the king. The ancient Persians followed an administrative system that resembled modern federal nation states!

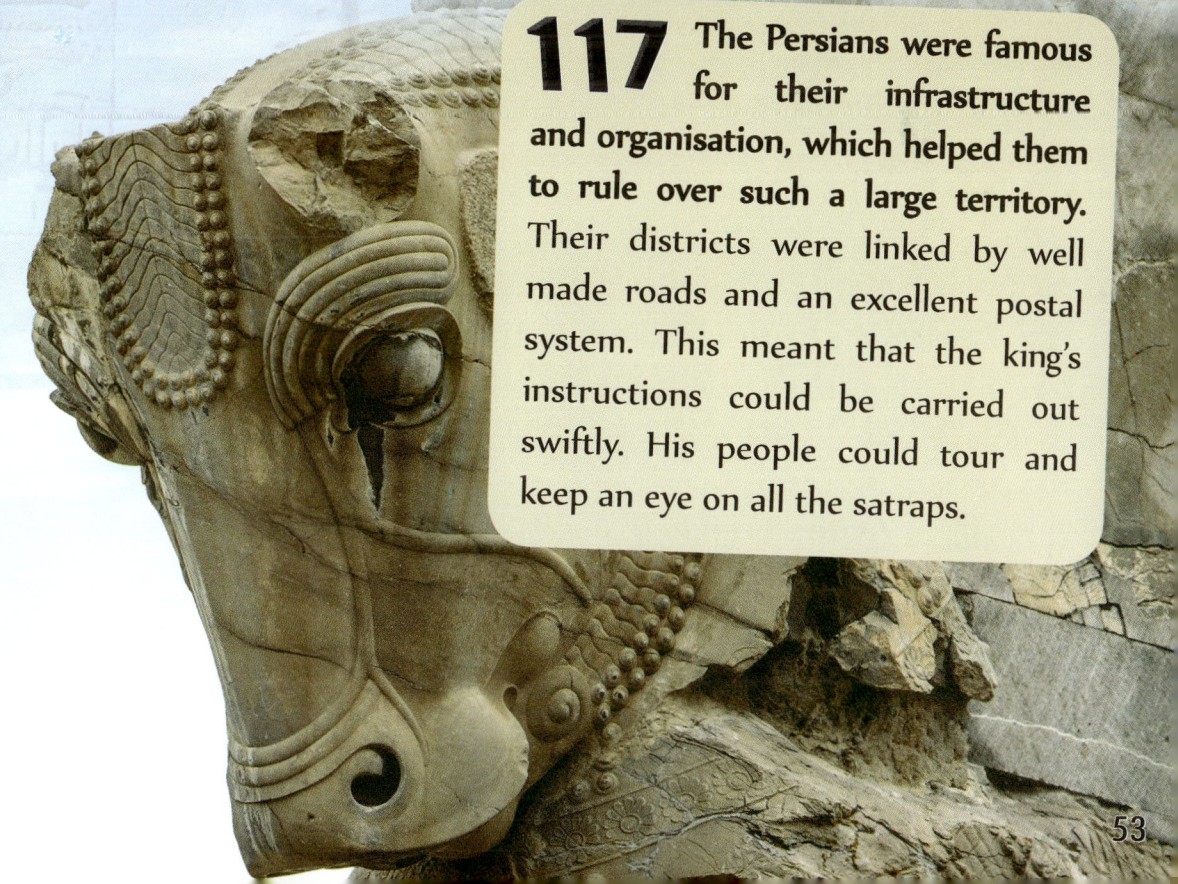

117 The Persians were famous for their infrastructure and organisation, which helped them to rule over such a large territory. Their districts were linked by well made roads and an excellent postal system. This meant that the king's instructions could be carried out swiftly. His people could tour and keep an eye on all the satraps.

EMPIRES

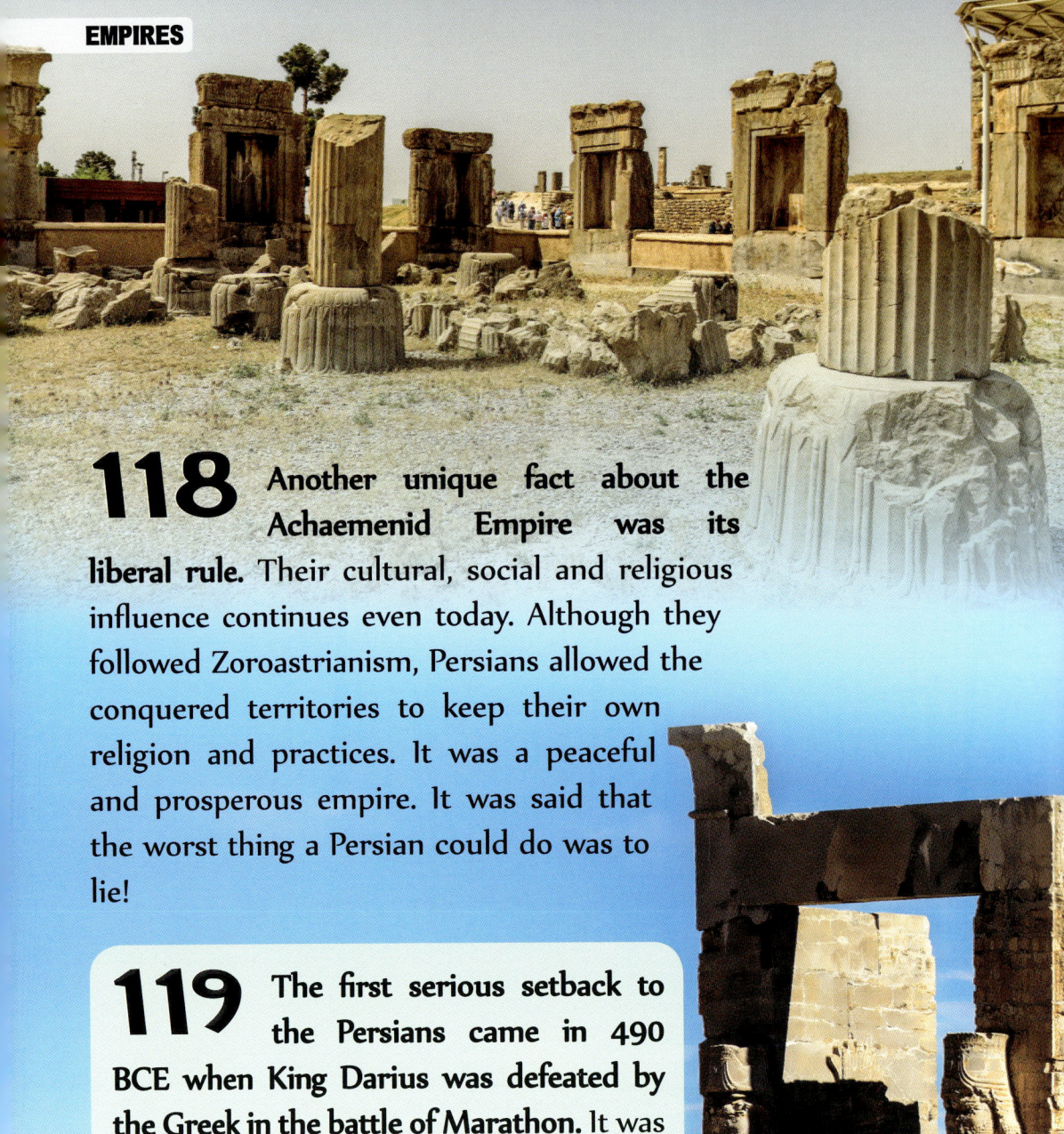

118 Another unique fact about the Achaemenid Empire was its liberal rule. Their cultural, social and religious influence continues even today. Although they followed Zoroastrianism, Persians allowed the conquered territories to keep their own religion and practices. It was a peaceful and prosperous empire. It was said that the worst thing a Persian could do was to lie!

119 The first serious setback to the Persians came in 490 BCE when King Darius was defeated by the Greek in the battle of Marathon. It was the first time the Greeks asserted their power. It was during this battle that the messenger Pheidippides is said to have run all the way from Marathon to Athens to give the news of their victory. This inspired the 'marathon' races that are run even today.

The Gate of All Nations in Persepolis, Iran.

THE CREATION OF EMPIRES

120 The Persian Empire was taken over by Alexander the Great when he defeated King Darius III in 333 BCE. Alexander was the king of Macedonia in northern Greece. He went on to conquer all of the eastern Mediterranean. By the age of 30, he had created the largest empire in the world, extending from Greece to north-western India.

121 Alexander's ambition took him to India in 327 BCE. But by this time his troops were exhausted with constant war. They wanted to return home and refused to go farther. Alexander was forced to turn back. On his return journey, Alexander fell sick in Babylon and died. His empire was then divided among his generals.

122 Around the same time, Chandragupta Maurya founded the Mauryan Empire in India, ruling from 322 to 185 BCE. After removing the ruling Nanda dynasty in the east, he took over Alexander's territories to the north. He created an empire that stretched over most of India and extended as far as Persia. It was one of the largest empires of its time.

EMPIRES

123 The Mauryan Empire was the first empire to unify most of India under a single rule. In this, Chandragupta Maurya was helped by the wily politician Chanakya or Kautilya, who helped in his political and economic rise. The empire was known for its strong administration, prosperous economy and safety. In fact, Chanakya's writings on politics and economics are considered one of India's greatest writings.

124 Like the Persians, the Mauryan Empire also had a strong central administration with an organised bureaucracy. We get a very clear and detailed description of the Mauryan idea of government from the Arthashastra written by Chanakya. Trade flourished as the Mauryan Empire built economic ties with powerful neighbours like Persia. Chandragupta later converted to Jainism. He then went into exile, leaving the empire to his son, Bindusara.

125 The Mauryan Empire reached its peak under Chandragupta Maurya's grandson, Ashoka the Great. He further strengthened the Mauryan Empire. He invaded and conquered Kalinga (modern day Odisha) in 261 BCE. But the destruction left by the war filled him with remorse and he refused to take up arms again.

THE CREATION OF EMPIRES

126 **Ashoka converted to Buddhism around 263 BCE, after the Kalinga war.** He dedicated his life to the spread of Buddhism. He is mainly responsible for its spread in Asia. His edicts on Buddhism, the right lifestyle and actions can still be seen carved on rock edicts. The capital of one such pillar, the Sarnath lion capital, is the national symbol of India.

127 **Ashoka is considered one of the greatest emperors in history.** His empire enjoyed a long period of political and social harmony. With many benevolent social policies, the Mauryan Empire under Ashoka is recognised as one of the most socially advanced kingdoms in the world. However, the Mauryan Empire collapsed shortly after his death.

128 **At this time in China, the Zhou Dynasty was the ruling power.** Lasting from 1046 to 256 BCE, it is the longest ruling Chinese dynasty. Their control over their territory was maintained through military might and alliances made through marriages. With time this control became weaker and the bordering city-states started to revolt.

EMPIRES

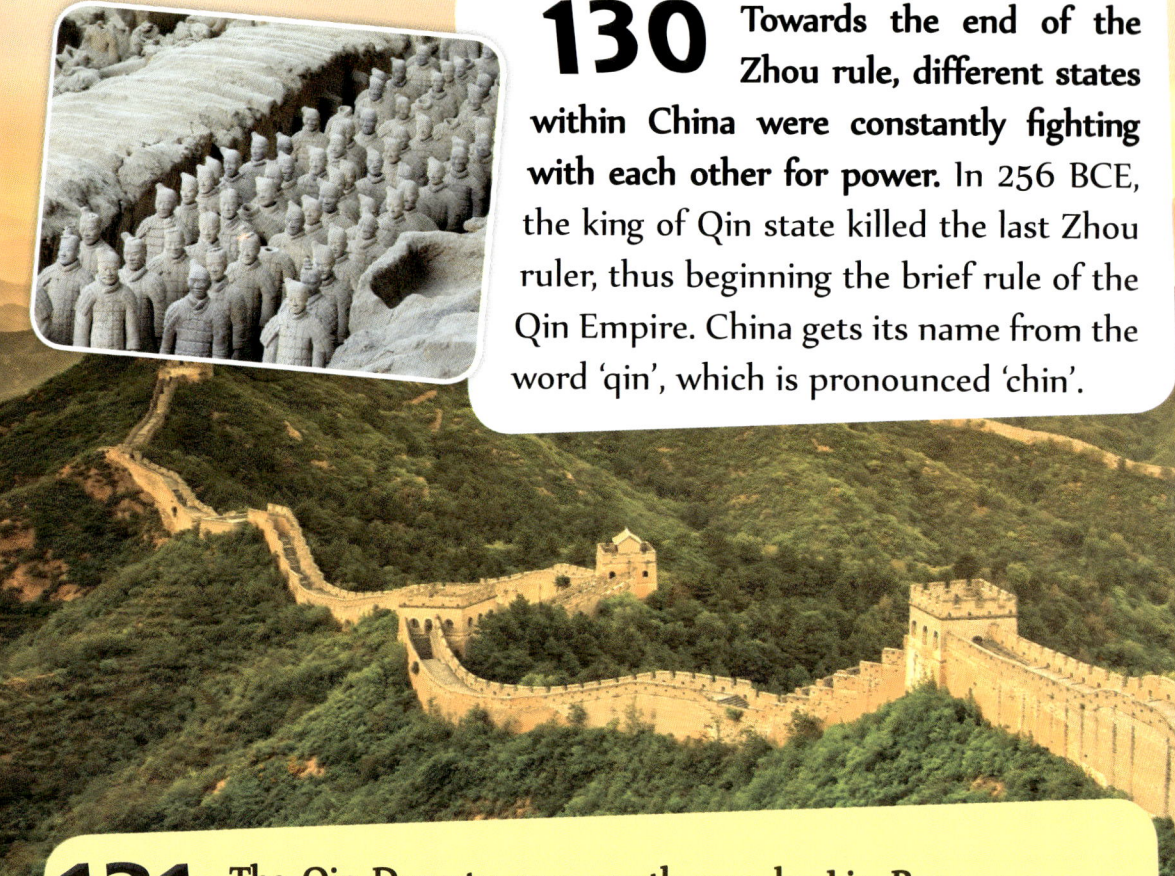

129 **The Zhou Dynasty had started unifying China, but it was never a strong empire.** It had too many challengers. But it is remembered as the golden age of Chinese philosophy. This is because many of China's great philosophies— Confucianism, Taoism, Mohism, etc., came to age at this time. These ideas and philosophies are still followed and respected throughout the world even today.

130 **Towards the end of the Zhou rule, different states within China were constantly fighting with each other for power.** In 256 BCE, the king of Qin state killed the last Zhou ruler, thus beginning the brief rule of the Qin Empire. China gets its name from the word 'qin', which is pronounced 'chin'.

131 **The Qin Dynasty was overthrown by Liu Bang, a peasant leader who was fed up with their brutal rule.** He changed his name to Han Gaozu and started the great Han Dynasty. It was the second imperial dynasty of China. The name 'Han' was inspired by the Han River, a tributary of the Yangtze River.

THE CREATION OF EMPIRES

132 The Qin Dynasty attempted to create a unified empire with clear political power. They also tried to stabilise the economy to support their military ambitions. The Qin dynasty's greatest contribution is its unification of China. It started and continued many infrastructure projects to create a great nation. One of these was the Great Wall of China!

133 The Han Dynasty maintained the boundaries established by the Qin Dynasty, keeping the great Chinese empire unified. Their rule lasted around 400 years, from 206 BCE to 220 CE. The Hans were challenged by a brief rebellion, which divided the Han rule into two parts—the Western Han (206 BCE – 9 CE) and the Eastern Han (25–220 CE).

The Great Wall of China was built in different areas by different dynasties.

EMPIRES

134 The Han Dynasty is counted among the most powerful and rich empires from the ancient world, rivalled only by the Romans in its influence on future generations. Their system of administration, culture and technological achievements left a profound impact on Chinese society. This period is also known as the Golden Age of Chinese history.

135 Trade and economy flourished under the Han Empire. Their currency system was followed for many years even after their rule ended. Despite its isolation, the Han Empire set up embassies in many other countries. This gave birth to one of the most important trade routes in the world—the Silk Route. It connected China, India, Persia and Europe.

The winding roads on old Silk Route, China.

THE CREATION OF EMPIRES

136

The Han Dynasty is also known for several technological advancements. Scientists and artists were held in high esteem and innovation was encouraged. As a result, China became a pioneer in many areas, such as agriculture, industry, mathematics, engineering and astronomy. These inventions and improvements continue to be important today. One such invention is paper.

137

The end of the Han Dynasty's reign started near the end of 1 CE when the emperor died without a chosen heir. This gave rise to a struggle for power within the ruling families. The feuding and corruption led to more instability. Finally, the Han rule ended in 220 CE. This plunged China into wars among states and warlords for the next 350 years.

138

In the West, it was a transformational time for the one of the greatest and most influential empires in history—the Roman Empire. The ideas, philosophies, inventions and governance of the empire would influence many future rulers and dynasties. Its impact can still be seen in the modern western civilisation.

EMPIRES

139 **Roman rule started with the Roman Republic, from 509 to 45 BCE.** It is termed a republic because its leaders, known as senators, were elected. Together they formed the Senate. This system of governance was very different from what had been followed by other ruling empires in the ancient world. It is still followed in many countries today, like in the USA!

140 **The Romans were a formidable military power.** The Roman Republic had evolved from the Roman kingdom. It soon spread its control over the entire Mediterranean region. It was one of the biggest empires in the world. But control over such a large area was extremely difficult. This gave rise to political and civil unrest, which kept the republic forever unstable.

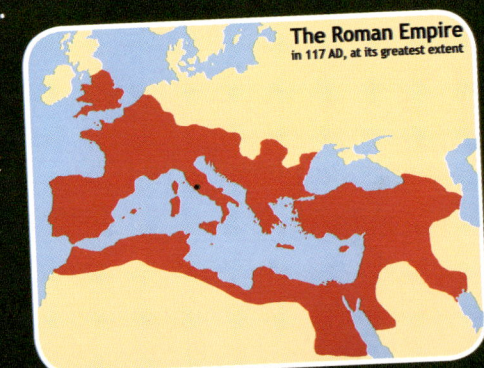

The Roman Empire in 117 AD, at its greatest extent

THE CREATION OF EMPIRES

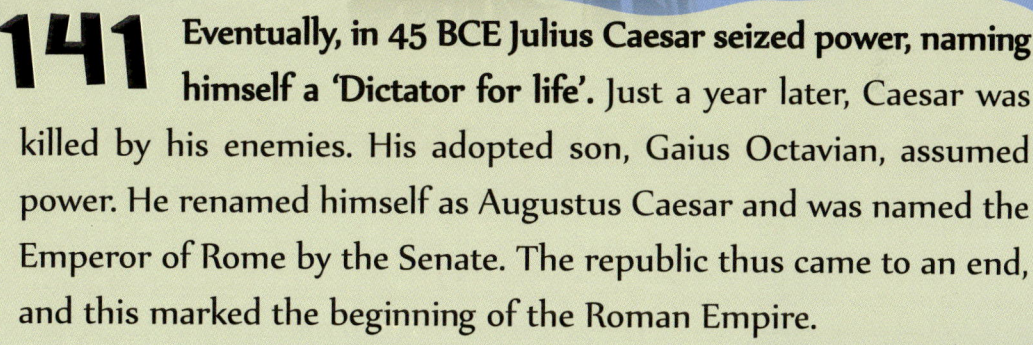

141 Eventually, in 45 BCE Julius Caesar seized power, naming himself a 'Dictator for life'. Just a year later, Caesar was killed by his enemies. His adopted son, Gaius Octavian, assumed power. He renamed himself as Augustus Caesar and was named the Emperor of Rome by the Senate. The republic thus came to an end, and this marked the beginning of the Roman Empire.

142 Augustus laid the foundation of the greatest empire in the world with law reforms, great works of art and culture, and a long period of peace and prosperity. Rome grew to be the most powerful and influential civilisation. The Roman Empire remained strong till 285 CE. By the end, it had become too large to be ruled and was broken up into two parts.

NEW WORLD

The Beginning (CE 1 - 400)

143 The Gregorian calendar, also known as western calendar, shifts directly from 31 December 1 BCE to 1 January 1 CE. This was because the concept of zero had not been introduced into the western world at the time when the calendar was first used.

144 The Christian era started with the crucifixion of Jesus in Judea. It is believed to have taken place between 30 to 33 CE. Archaeologists have recovered some artefacts from that period, but there are very few architectural remains. However, some carvings in stone have been found, which seem to have followed the Roman style of art.

145 The Chinese Emperor Kuang Wu Ti founded Han Dynasty (206 BCE-220 CE) which was one of the longest lasting empires in history. Significant developments in economy, science and technology took place, including paper making, development of the nautical steering rudder, use of negative numbers in maths, etc. Buddhism was also introduced in China during this time.

THE BEGINNING (CE 1 - 400)

146 **The great fire of Rome took place in July 64 CE.** It took six days to control the fire. It is suggested that the fire was ordered by Roman Emperor Nero to clear land to build his planned palatial complex 'The Domus Aurea'. However, Nero blamed the small Christian community in the city for the fire!

147 **The Colosseum in Rome is also known as the Coliseum or the Flavian Amphitheatre.** It was built under the rule of three rulers of the Flavian Dynasty—Vespasian, Titus, and Domitian. It was used as a public arena where an average of 65,000 spectators could view dramas, executions, and animal battles. It continues to be an iconic symbol of imperial Rome.

> Colosseum in Rome was commissioned by Emperor Vespasian as a gift to the Roman people.

148 **Despite the opposition from the Roman Empire, Christianity grew steadily in popularity.** This was helped by the energetic and devout evangelists who shared the word of Christ and converted people to the new faith. The gospels of four Evangelists—St. Mathew, St. Mark, St. Luke and St John—were recorded as part of the New Testament of the Bible.

NEW WORLD

149 **The Roman Emperor Hadrian (117-138) nationalised the postal system.** Horse driven mail carts, horseback carriers and postal coaches were used, and well engineered roads were laid. There were post relay stations at intervals, with station masters, accountants, grooms for horses, and mail carriers.

cursus publicus

150 **The Silk route was a trade route that developed during the Han Dynasty, linking China with Europe.** Many goods of great and small value were traded along the many smaller trading posts and cities along the route. Silk was an exotic and rare material, as at the time no one except the Chinese knew the secret to making silk. It was so costly that it was valued in gold! The Romans thought that silk might be a vegetable product obtained from trees.

151 **One of the important trades that existed at the time was the spice trade.** Spices like pepper, turmeric, ginger, cardamom and cinnamon which grew on the Indian peninsula and in South-East Asia were in great demand in many parts of Europe and North-East Africa. There is evidence that there were strong trade links between Rome and southern Indian kingdoms in the first century CE.

THE BEGINNING (CE 1 - 400)

152 **The ancient Indian kingdoms used the Saka system of dating as a calendar.** The term 'Shaka' in Sanskrit was used for the Central Asian invaders, who ruled over parts of North India around the first century CE. It is believed that it marks either the defeat of the Shaka Kings, or the beginning of their rule. It begins from the year 78 CE of the western calendar.

153 **The city of Peshawar in present day Pakistan shows signs of continuous habitation from as far back as 540 BCE.** It was earlier known as Purushpur. The city was captured by Emperor Kanishka around 120 CE. This city had earlier passed through the hands of Alexander, his successors, Seleucus Nicator and then Chandragupta Maurya.

154 **Halley's comet was first reported to have been observed in 240 BCE.** It then appeared in 164 BCE, 87 BCE, 12 BCE and then in 66 CE, and was recorded by the Chinese, Mesopotamians and Europeans. However, they did not recognise that it was the same comet returning. It is a periodic comet and returns to the vicinity of the Earth every 75 years. It was reported during the Han Dynasty as the 'Kou Sing', which means the 'visiting star' in Chinese.

NEW WORLD

155 Hatra is an ancient Arab city located near Baghdad in Iraq. It is known as the 'City of the Sun God' after the Temple of Shamash, which was one of its main structures. It was developed by the son of the Nasr Emperor, Sanatruq, in 146 CE. The city is guarded by two walls that can be crossed by ascending up ramps which run parallel to the wall.

156 The fortress of Van in present day eastern Turkey was built as a fortification during the ninth to seventh century BCE. It was an important fortress and each ruling power in the area tried to gain control over it, including the Achaemenids and Romans. The fortress has an inscription by Persian King Xerxes, in three languages. This helped to decipher the cuneiform alphabet. Today, only a handful qualified cuneiformists are there throughout the world.

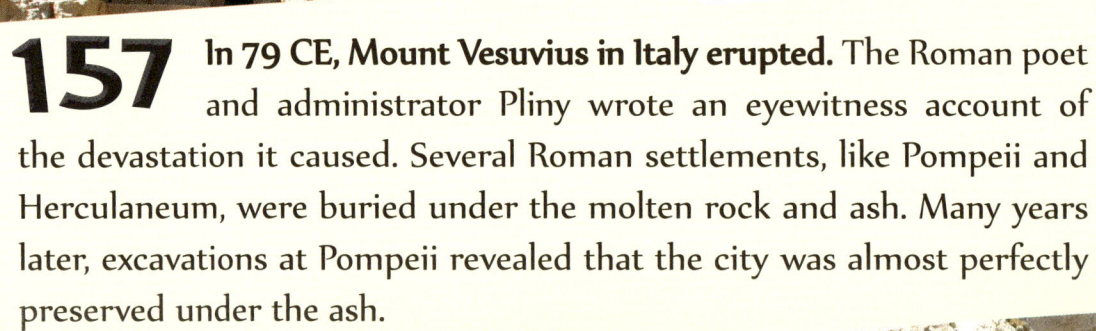

157 In 79 CE, Mount Vesuvius in Italy erupted. The Roman poet and administrator Pliny wrote an eyewitness account of the devastation it caused. Several Roman settlements, like Pompeii and Herculaneum, were buried under the molten rock and ash. Many years later, excavations at Pompeii revealed that the city was almost perfectly preserved under the ash.

THE BEGINNING (CE 1 - 400)

158 **The Caspian or Caucasian Leopard was almost hunted to extinction by the Romans.** These animals were often captured and made to fight in the Coliseum of Rome, either against each other, or against humans known as gladiators.

Naqsh-e Rostam, tomb of Persian kings in Iran.

159 **The Canal of the Pharaohs was a link between the Nile and the Red Sea.** It was supposedly started by the Pharaohs, and further developed under the Persian King Darius. However, most of the evidence point out that he was not able to complete the canal and it was finally finished around 270 BCE. Later, by the second century CE, the Romans cleared this canal and it came to be known as the River of Trajan.

160 **Rome was hit by a plague in 165-180 CE.** It was known as the Antotine plague or the Plague of Galen. It was brought back to the city by troops returning from the Near-East. The Greek physician Galen wrote about the outbreak, and based on his descriptions, scholars believe this might have been an epidemic of smallpox.

NEW WORLD

161
The Chinese Han Dynasty came to an end in the early second century (190-220 CE). One of the major events leading to this was the 'Yellow Turban Turmoil'. This was a peasant rebellion against the Han rulers that lasted from 184-205 CE. Though the Han forces ultimately crushed the rebellion, the local leaders had gained a lot of power, and the Han rule was badly weakened.

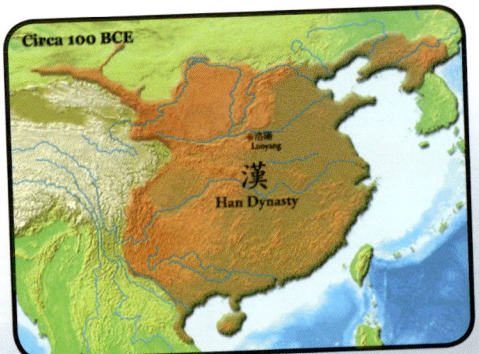

162
Chinese literature mentions the oldest recorded supernova observed by humans, in 185 CE. The Supernova was termed 'Guest star' in Chinese literature and said to look like a 'giant bamboo mat'. It took about eight months to fade away.

THE BEGINNING (CE 1 - 400)

163 **Mt. Taupo, New Zealand started erupting about 3,00,000 years ago.** The most violent eruption of this volcano took place in 186 CE, and is known as the Hatepe eruption. It unleashed about 30 km³ ash and lava at the rate of 900 km/hr. It was such a violent eruption that the sky was recorded to have turned red as far away as Rome and China.

Mount Taupo, New Zealand.

NEW WORLD

164 Gunpowder was invented by Chinese alchemists in early 200 CE. It is listed as one of the four great inventions of China. It is the first propellant and physical explosive devised by humans. It is recorded that Wei Boyang discovered its properties in 142 CE, who called it a powder that could fly and dance.

165 Rome was attacked by waves of nomadic warriors from the East from 238 CE. These attackers were termed 'barbarians' by the Romans. The attacks continued over hundreds of years, with large scale attacks taking place in the early 400 CE. One of the most important of these attacks was the one led by King Alaric of the Visigoths in 410 CE. They plundered and looted Rome, but did not hurt or torture the inhabitants.

166 Ardashir I, or 'Ardashir the unifier' was the founder of the Sassanian Empire. It spread from Syria and Turkey in the west, to most of Central Asia in the east. The Sassanian Empire was constantly battling against the Roman Empire to the west. It had a very strong cultural influence in the region and beyond.

167 Marcus Julius Phillipus was the Roman Emperor from 244-249 CE. He was also known as Phillip the Arab. He wanted to make peace with the Persians, and thus struck coins stating: 'PAX FUNDATA CUM PERSIS', which means, 'Peace founded with Persia'.

THE BEGINNING (CE 1 - 400)

168 The Library of Alexandria in north Egypt was one of the largest and most important libraries of the ancient world. It was initially built by a student of Aristotle in the third century BCE, but continued to be a centre of scholarship until at least 642 CE. It is also believed to have been burned down by the Roman armies in the intervening centuries. However, it it is not clear if there was just one fire or whether there were a number of fires over time that destroyed it.

169 The Kingdom of Armenia was the first nation to make Christianity its state religion in 301 CE. This was followed by the Edict of Milan in the Roman Empire in 313 CE, to legalise Christianity. Before that, Christianity was usually followed by poor people and was banned by the rich.

170 The Dunhuand caves in China are also known as the Magao caves. They are a system of 492 temples located at the religious and cultural crossroads on the Silk Route, in Ghansu province. These grottos were constructed around 366 CE and are the largest Buddhist caves in the world.

NEW WORLD

171 **The Nabataeans were Arab people who had a well established trade route that linked one oasis to another in north Arabia and the Levant.** Their capital was the city of Raqmu, which later came to be known as Petra. In the first century CE, they became allies of Rome. An earthquake in 363 CE destroyed the city and crippled the vital water management system. Nearly half of the city was destroyed because of this event.

172 **Theodosius 1 (379-395 CE) was the last Roman Emperor to rule over both Eastern and Western halves of the Empire.** He campaigned against Goths and other barbarians invading the city but failed to defeat them. He banned the pagan rituals of the Greek Olympics in 393 CE. He also made Christianity the official state religion of Rome.

RELIGIOUS HISTORY

Religious World (400-800 CE)

173 By 400 CE, most parts of the world had experienced some form of civilisation. Trade played an important role in improving communication between different empires. All the civilisations were now growing crops, such as maize, wheat and sweet potatoes. Mining of gold, silver, and copper was also useful, not only for making tools, implements and weapons, but also for trade. Along with goods, religions also spread along the trade routes.

174 In South America, during this period, the Tiahuanaco Empire was the most important political entity. It also provided a religious centre for the people. At its height, the empire was spread over most of Bolivia, as well as Chile and Peru. Archaeological study of the site of Tiahuanaco has revealed many impressive stone structures, including a massive gate carved from a single rock, known as the 'Gateway of the Sun'. A submerged temple has also been found in nearby Lake Titicaca.

RELIGIOUS HISTORY

175 Around 300 BCE to 700 CE, a group of people lived along the banks of Mississippi river. This Native American community was later termed as the 'Hopewell culture'. This society produced beautiful artwork, most of which seems to have had religious purposes. Many of these have been recovered from graves, which are often found filled with necklaces, carvings, decorated pottery, and even woven mats. From the grave goods, it is clear that they believed in some form of life after death.

Pyramids in Teotihuacan, Mexico.

176 The city of Teotihuacan was located in the Mexico valley. Around 250 CE, it was a flourishing religious centre with a large population, but it seems to have declined around 550 CE. The city had several temples, many of which have been excavated and studied by archaeologists in recent years. The people of this region had a well developed cosmology and myth system, and prayed to a number of Gods and Goddesses, such as the Great Goddess, the Storm God, and so on. Evidence of both animal and human sacrifice has been found here.

RELIGIOUS WORLD (400-800 CE)

177 **Polynesian people spread across the islands of the Pacific Ocean.** They were skilful navigators and used to travel huge distances by observing the movements of the stars, wave patterns and changes in the wind pattern. They used to carry men, women, children, animals and seeds to start new lives on the islands they reached. They believed in life after death and their religion focused more on nature spirits and deities.

178 **Do you know that Hawaii and other islands near it were very fertile and were good for growing crops?** Polynesian sailors went through all of these islands and some of them settled there. They built platforms of stones in these islands and used them for religious ceremonies.

RELIGIOUS HISTORY

179 The Mayan civilisation developed over thousands of years, but its Classical period is identified as lasting from 250 CE to the ninth century. In the Classical period, the Mayans developed the idea of a Divine King who acted as mediator between Gods and humans.

180 The Mayans invented two calendars. One was the accurate yearly calendar of 365 days which was made according to the revolution of the Earth around the sun. The other was the sacred calendar of 260 days, used to predict the future and avoid bad luck. Only Mayan priests were able to read this calendar.

181 In the lives of Mayan people, religion played an important role. The style of the temple-pyramids of Maya was copied from temples at Teotihuacan. Mayan cities were controlled by priests as well as lords. One of the most famous temples of the Mayans was the Temple of Tikal, or the Temple of the Great Jagaur. It was named this because it has a carving representing a ruler seated on a jaguar throne.

Mayan ruins of Temple of Tikal, Guatemala.

RELIGIOUS WORLD (400-800 CE)

182 **During the fifth and sixth century CE, in southern England the Angles, Saxons and Jutes worshipped their own gods.** A Christian monk of the Benedictine order, Augustine, landed in England in 597 CE. He was appointed to take 40 monks to England to convert people to Christianity. Augustine was the founder of the English Church, and became the first Archbishop of Canterbury in 597 CE.

183 **The main aim of the Roman Empire under Emperor Justinian was to unite the Eastern and Western Christian Empires.** To achieve this aim he ordered his armies to attack barbarian kingdoms. After 565 CE, his armies conquered North Africa and most of Italy. One of his most important contributions was the civil code known as the Code of Justinian. This was mainly a combination of previous law codes, and it had a great influence on later European laws.

184 **Attila was a great leader of the Huns from 434 to 453 CE.** The Huns settled near the shores of the Danube, from where they attacked Gaul and Rome. Attila attacked both the Eastern and Western Roman Empires. He died in 453 CE, and gradually the Huns were assimilated into the population of Europe. Over the next few centuries, they adopted Christianity.

RELIGIOUS HISTORY

185 **When the Roman Empire broke up, the eastern half came to be known as the Byzantine Empire.** This empire was very prosperous, and Byzantine gold coins were made and valued for over 700 years. At that time, the only people who could read or write in Byzantine were monks and scholars. Books were handwritten and illustrated. It took many months to create one book.

186 **Do you know about the Dark Ages?** Because there was no longer a large centre of art and culture, it was believed that Europe had fallen into a Dark Age. However, there was actually a lot of regional art that flourished at this time. Christianity also spread all over the continent during this time.

187 **Europe split into many smaller kingdoms after the decline of Rome.** The Frankish ruler, Charles Martel defeated the Arab armies of Spain in 732 CE. Later in 768 CE, Charlemagne, the grandson of Charles Martel, was made King of Franks. His main aim was to spread Christianity. He encouraged education, improved the legal system of the areas he conquered and even helped build monasteries.

RELIGIOUS WORLD (400-800 CE)

188 Prophet Mohammad was born in Mecca about 570 CE. He and his early followers migrated from Mecca to Medina in 622 CE. This event was known as the Hijra. The Islamic calendar (also called Hijri calendar) begins from this date.

189 Prophet Mohammed is credited with not only the founding of Islam but also of uniting Arabia into a single polity.

190 The Mosque of the Dome of the Rock in Jerusalem is believed to be one of the earliest existing Islamic buildings. It was completed in 691 CE by the Umayyid Caliph.

RELIGIOUS HISTORY

191 After Prophet Muhammad's death, his son in law, Abu Bakr, became the successor and chief defender of Islam. However, he too died soon after, in 634 CE. He was followed by Umar, Usman and Ali. These four successors of Muhammad are said to constitute the Rashidun Caliphate. By that time, almost all of Arabia began to follow Islam.

192 Muawiya became the first Umayyid Caliph in 661 CE. He ruled for 20 years, and established his capital in Damascus. Under his rule, the armies of Islam spread far and wide, converting people both westward towards Europe and eastward into Central Asia.

193 The Umayyids were followed by the Abbasid Caliphs. In 762 CE, the Abbasids shifted their capital from Damascus to Baghdad and built a beautiful city there. It soon emerged as a centre of learning, with many schools and a university. Baghdad also became the centre of a huge trading empire, as many goods like copper, camphor, amber and jewellery were carried to and from Basra.

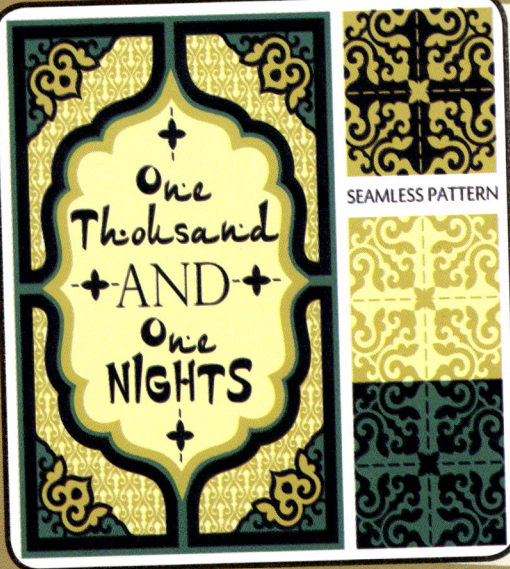

194 The *Arabian Nights* are a series of 1,001 tales written in the Arabic language. It was originally known as *Alf Laila wa Laila*. It is believed that some of the descriptions in the stories were inspired by the court of the most famous Abbasid Caliph, Haroun al Rashid.

RELIGIOUS WORLD (400-800 CE)

195 **Today, Islam is one of the world's largest religions, with more than 1.6 billion followers of all colours, nations and race.** Islam reached the shores of India as early as the seventh century CE with the Arab traders. It was much later, in the 12th century that an Islamic state was established under the Delhi Sultanate in North India.

196 **The Koran is the holy book of Muslims.** It is believed that it records the direct words of Allah as revealed to Prophet Mohammed. Muslims celebrate the revelation of the Koran to the Prophet by observing a month of fasting. During this period, known as Ramzan, Muslims typically try to cover a complete recitation of the Koran.

RELIGIOUS HISTORY

197 **During the fifth century CE, the Japanese were under the influence of the Chinese.** The Japanese were taught how to read and write Chinese by Buddhist monks. Around 538 CE, the old Japanese temples were replaced by new Buddhist temples. Gradually, the Chinese influenced Japan to adopt Buddhism as their official religion.

198 **China's 'Golden Age' is believed to have started in 618 CE with the Tang dynasty, and continued under the Song Dynasty (960-1279 CE).** It was a period in which there were many new inventions, such as printing on paper using moveable wooden type. The people were largely Buddhist, though there was a strong influence of Confucian ideas.

It was the Chinese that brought Buddhism to Japan.

RELIGIOUS WORLD (400-800 CE)

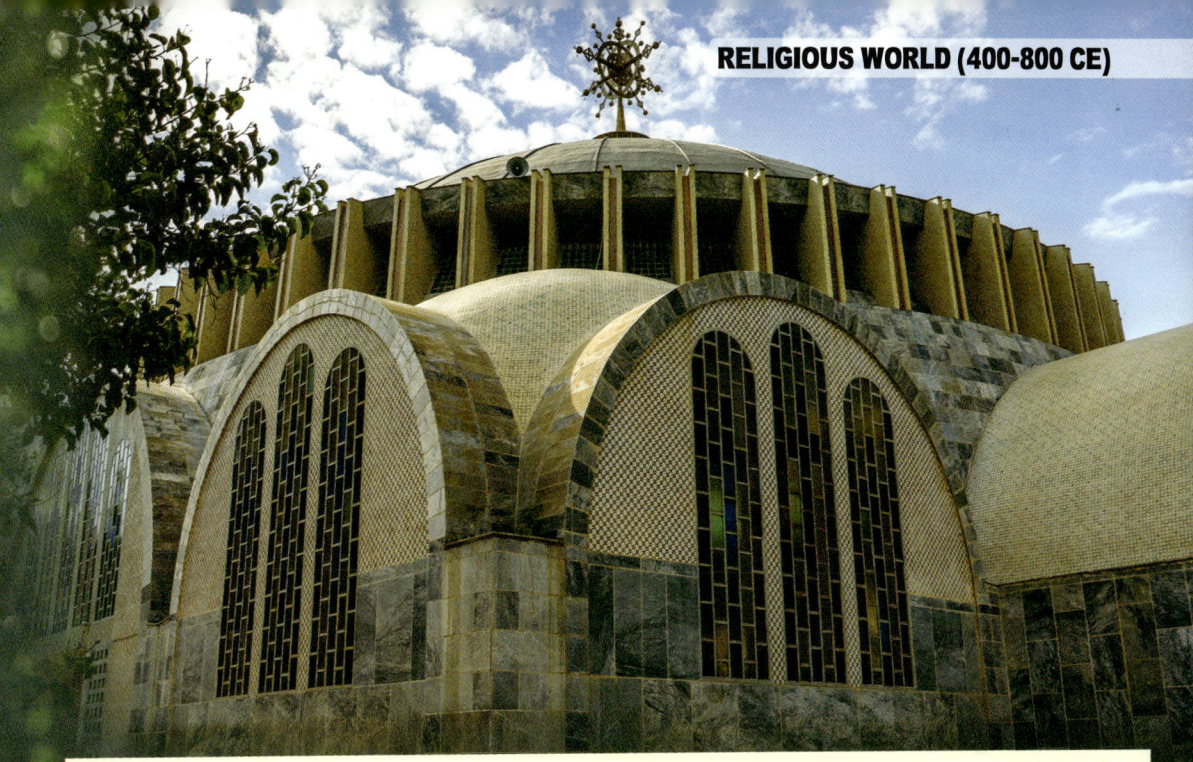

199 The people of the Aksum Empire in Northeast Africa used to worship their own gods till the 300s, but after one of their ruler King Ezana became Christian, most of the people of the country started following the new religion as well.

200 The kingdom of Ghana in West Africa was known as 'the land of gold' because its wealth came from its rich gold mines. This was exported across the Saharan Caravan routes as gold dust in place of copper, cotton and salt. The traditional religion of Ghana saw gods as intermediaries between humans and the Supreme Being. They believed that deceased ancestors could help them, and thus, honoured them as well.

Medieval Period

201 The phrase 'middle ages' or 'medieval period' is used to describe the historical period that followed the ancient period. In Europe it covered the period between fifth century CE, when the Roman Empire declined, and the Renaissance, which began in 14th century CE. Most historians and scholars prefer to use the phrase 'medieval period' instead of 'middle ages' because the word 'period' implies an era which holds some significance.

202 The beginning of the medieval period in some parts of the world, such as Asia, Africa and Americas is given slightly different dates. In some cases, it is also divided between early medieval period and later medieval period. Between sixth century CE and 12th century CE, India saw a number of powerful regional kingdoms and this period is known as the early medieval age. Between 12th century CE and 17th century CE, it went through the later medieval period, before transitioning to the modern period.

MEDIEVAL PERIOD

203 The term 'medieval' is derived from the Latin words 'medium aevum' which literally translates to 'middle ages'. Sometimes, the early middle ages or medieval period in Europe is referred to as the Dark Ages. It is called so because this period was marked by frequent warfare leading to demographic, cultural and economic deterioration. The idea of using 'dark' is to contrast it with the 'light' of the later periods. But the whole of the medieval period in Europe was one fraught with danger and devastation.

204 Historical research shows that the biggest killer during this period was the plague. It had a detrimental effect on the population of Europe in the 14th and 15th centuries. The plague was caused by a bacterium called yersinia pestis and because of the deaths it caused, it was also known as the Black Death. It is estimated that the Black Death killed a third and half of Europe's population.

205 Another surprising and big killer during this period was travel. When travelling, people faced many threats. They had to find a safe and clean place to sleep, especially during the winters. Unless the travellers found an inn or a monastery to stay in, they had to struggle for food and drink. In any case, even finding a place to stay at night could be risky with high incidents of food poisoning.

RELIGIOUS HISTORY

206 Between 1315 and 1322, Europe witnessed heavy rainfall, sometimes lasting up to 150 days at a time. This was accompanied by the 'Great Famine' and climate change which led to colder temperatures. Which is why, this period is called the 'Little Ice Age'. Dwindling food supplies, poor harvests, and illnesses, such as tuberculosis, sweating sickness, smallpox, and dysentery, marked the early 14th century. In England at least 10 per cent of the population died during this period.

The Great Famine represented in a painting.

207 During the medieval period, giving birth was a perilous and hazardous process. Many women died during child birth, either due to long labour pains and exhaustion, or infection. Even though caesarean sections were known, they were not that common and in most cases ended in the death of either the child or the mother. In 1537, Jane Seymour, the third wife of Henry VIII, died soon after giving birth to their son, Edward VI.

208 Even if children survived their birth, not many lived up to adulthood. Infants and children below seven were vulnerable to malnutrition, diseases and infections. The majority of those killed by the Black Death or plague were children. Being born into a wealthy family did not guarantee a long life. Between 1330 and 1479, one-third children from the English aristocrat families died before the age of five.

MEDIEVAL PERIOD

209 **Medieval period in Europe is known for its sumptuous meals and culinary inventions.** Curye on Inglysch is a manuscript found from the 14th century containing culinary recipes of many dishes which are considered gourmet cuisines in contemporary times. One of them is a recipe for a sweet and sour rabbit. The recipe included sugar, red wine vinegar, currants, onions, ginger and cinnamon. All these were used to make a sticky sauce served with rabbit.

210 **The use of pastry was very common in medieval times and most food was wrapped in it.** These pastries allowed various kinds of meat to be cooked in stone ovens without the fear of being burnt or over cooked. They were protected from the soot as well. Pastries were elaborately decorated to show off  the status of the person hosting the meal, and would be discarded by the guests to get to the filling.

211 **One of the largest empires of this period was the Ottoman Empire.** Also known as the Turkish Empire, it was founded at the end of the 13th century and reached its height of power during the 16th and 17th centuries under Suleiman the Magnificent. As a vast, multilingual empire, it controlled most of southeast Europe, central Europe, western Asia, eastern Europe and north Africa. By the beginning of 17th century, it comprised 32 provinces and numerous vassal states.

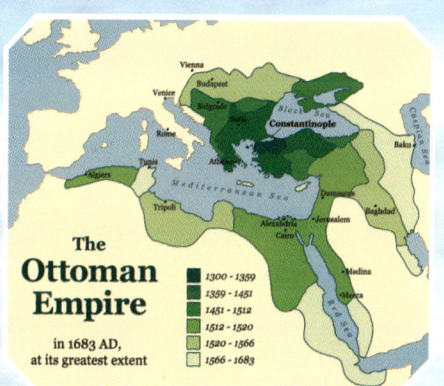

RELIGIOUS HISTORY

212 **Suleiman the Magnificent ruled from 1494 to 1566.** He created a uniform system of law. For this, he was given the title 'Kanui Sultan Suleiman' which translates to the 'Lawgiver Suleiman'. He also patronised different forms of art and literature.

213 **The Ottomans built a strong political and military system that was very similar to the Romans.** For instance, before any military campaign, the military commanders consulted old soldiers, war experts and war records. Then, they gathered and stored food and armaments which were complemented by live produce collected from designated villages along their campaign routes. Around the same time, scouts were sent out to find the best possible routes for entering the enemy territory. Finally, infrastructure like roads and bridges were made stronger to support the marching army.

Battle of Mohacs, 1526, Ottoman victory over Hungary.

214 **The Ottoman army imposed a strict and fierce discipline on its soldiers.** These included frugal food habits, and proper sanitation measures inside the camp. Such measures actually mitigated camp diseases and curbed rowdy behaviour among the men. Strict training schedules, strenuous exercises, like horse archery, were a systemic part of the soldiers' trainings. In fact, many contemporary European observers were amazed by both the quietness and the discipline inside the Ottoman army camps.

MEDIEVAL PERIOD

215 The humble sipahi or the foot soldier played the greatest role in Ottoman military. These soldiers were paid a fief or land instead of a regular salary. This land was handed over to them in trust, but without any corresponding rights over either the land or the farmers who worked on it. Written records show that the sipahi was supposed to pay the farmers who would work on his land. The sipahi was a formidable foe not only because of his mobility on the battle field, but also because he could double as an expert horseman.

216 By 16th century, the Ottomans had incorporated a number of arms in their army that made tactical use of cavalry, infantry and artillery. These combined arms were organised in a classic battle tactic. The main body of the army entrenched themselves in field fortifications, gun wagons and ditches. In the centre of this body stood the Sultan surrounded by the elite military force. On both sides of this were the cavalry; while to the front and the rear of the artillery stood the infantry and the sipahi who were armed with bows, axes and swords.

217 The Ottomans were excellent at artillery-based warfare and gun powder weaponry. They had giant canons with modular designs which allowed them to be assembled on the battlefield. Some of these guns were capable of shooting over a mile with a capacity of firing a 1,000-pound ball. These guns allowed the Ottomans to break massive defence structures giving them the edge in attacks.

RELIGIOUS HISTORY

218 In 1323 the empire reached the Black Sea when they captured Karamursel. The first Ottoman naval shipyard was set up here and the Ottoman fleet was established. Later, Karamursel would become the nucleus of this navy. The navy extended all the way to the Indian Ocean when the Ottomans sent an expedition to Indonesia in 1565.

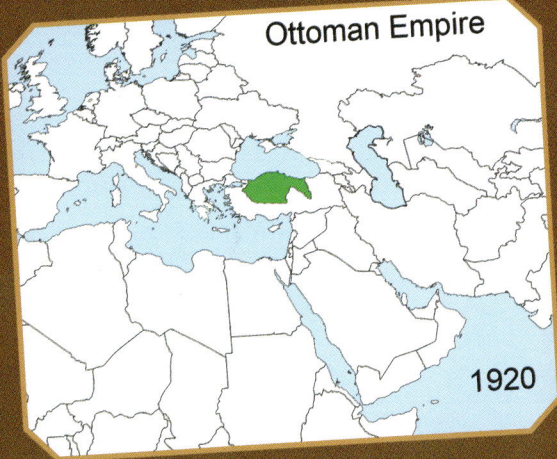

219 The Ottoman Empire would formally decline and cease to exist in 1923, which means it lasted for 634 years. But its decline had already begun in the 18th and 19th century with the rise of other powerful empires in Europe.

220 The Republic of Turkey was founded on the remnants of the fallen Ottoman Empire on 29 October 1923. Mustafa Kemal Pasha was the founder of the new Turkish state and went on to serve as its first president from 1923 until his death in 1938.

MEDIEVAL PERIOD

221 **The Indian subcontinent saw a lot of political and economic activity during the medieval period.** But it is particularly known for its rich religious history during this time. Sikhism, the fifth largest organised religion in the world, with approximately 30 million followers was founded in India in the 15th century. It originated in the Punjab region but soon spread slowly over the subcontinent. It is the youngest of the major world religions.

222 **Sikhism is a monotheistic religion.** Its teachings emphasise that God is indescribable, has no shape and no gender. Ek Omkar is used as a symbol to represent the one supreme and true reality which sometimes also translates into as 'one with everything'.

223 **The founder of Sikhism was Guru Nanak, the first of the 10 Sikh gurus.** He was born in 1496 in Nankana Sahib which is in present day Pakistan. His teachings included meditating on the name of the creator, engaging in selfless service, helping others, and leading an honest life.

RELIGIOUS HISTORY

224 It was the fifth guru, Guru Arjan who set out to compile the teachings of all the gurus into a scripture, Guru Granth Sahib. After Guru Arjan the successive gurus added their teachings to the text. The tenth and final Guru of the Sikhs, Guru Gobind Singh, told his followers that after his death there would be no more living gurus. Instead, the Sikhs were supposed to live according to the teachings compiled in the Guru Granth Sahib.

225 This region is also famous for its flurry of activity associated with the construction of temples. There were two predominant styles that emerged after the fall of the Gupta Empire in India in the seventh century. They are categorised into the north Indian style and the south Indian style.

226 The north Indian style temples generally have a high tower called the shikhara and an open porch called the mandapa. Like the earlier Roman temples, the roofs were flat and made of stone.

227 Like the north Indian temples, the south Indian temples too had a shikhara or tower. The difference was in the height of the shikharas. Those found in South India are higher, sometimes going up as high as 13 storeys. They even have many mandapas. The sculptures too are more elaborate.

MEDIEVAL PERIOD

228 Raja Raja a ruler of the Chola kingdom, commissioned the construction of the Brihadeeswarar Temple. It was completed in 1010 CE and is now also known as the Raja Rajeswara Temple. Located in Thanjavur, it is dedicated to Lord Shiva and is part of the UNESCO World Heritage Site. It shares the status of the 'Great Living Chola Temples' with Gangaikonda Cholapuram Temple and the Airavatesvara Temple.

229 Humayun's tomb and the Taj Mahal are other examples of architectural marvel which were constructed in the later part of the medieval period. While Humayun's tomb was commissioned by his wife Haji Begum after his death in 1556, the building of Taj Mahal was decreed by Shah Jahan in the memory of his deceased wife Mumtaz Mahal in 1632.

230 Most of these tombs were placed in a perfect quadrilateral garden layout called Chahar Bagh. They symbolised the four gardens of paradise mentioned in the Koran. These gardens were divided by canals of water, which all met at a basin or a fountain.

ART AND CULTURE

History of Art and Culture

231 **Ikebana or Kado is the Japanese art of flower arrangement.** Ikebana means 'giving life to flowers' and Kado means 'the way of flowers'. The earliest records of this art form can be seen in the *Kao irai no Kadensho*, an Ikebana manuscript that dates back to 1486 CE. However, the art form seems to have originated much earlier around 538 CE, when Buddhist monks started arranging flowers to decorate temple altars!

232 **Leon Battista Alberti (1404-1472 CE), the Italian architect and humanist scholar wrote three treatises: On Painting, On Architecture and On Sculpture, which were vital contributions to the respective fields.** Alberti was one of the first Renaissance architects to apply classical elements in structures designed by him after thoroughly understanding their purpose. His most notable work is the Palazzo Rucellai in Florence.

233 **Chanoyu ('hot water for tea') is a Japanese tea ceremony.** It was brought to Japan from China in the 15th century CE by a Zen priest named Shukō, who is also known as the father of Chanoyu. According to Okakura Kakuzo, 'The whole ideal of [chadō (way of tea)] is a result of this Zen conception of greatness in the smallest incidents of life.'

HISTORY OF ART AND CULTURE

234 **Pir Budaq, governor of Baghdad and famous ruler of Qara Quyunlu from 1455-1460 CE, was also a notable patron of the arts.** He invited artists from around the eastern Islamic world to bring together styles of Tabriz and Shiraz in Iran and Timurid in Central Asia. His violent death at the hands of his father brought an end to an epoch period in which art and culture had flourished in Baghdad.

235 ***Très Riches Heures du duc de Berry* is one of the best examples of the French style of manuscript illustration.** It is a painting using ink on vellum, and was probably painted between 1412 and 1416 CE, by the brothers Herman, Paul, and Jean de Limbourg. A notable feature of the painting is the portrait of the patron, Jean de France, Duc de Berry in a blue robe on the opposite side of the table in the painting. Unfortunately, the painters died in 1416, possibly due to plague. The painting was later completed by another artist in the 1440s.

236 **The Ming Dynasty was the last notable dynasty of China under which the kingdom flourished in the fields of navigation, Confucianism and art.** The famous Forbidden City was created at this time—an imperial palace renowned for its opulence. The Ming established three schools of painting—Che, Wu and the Eccentric style, reflecting spontaneity and freedom of expression.

ART AND CULTURE

237 **The Gutenberg Press was named after Johannes Gutenberg, the inventor of printing press process.** This marked an defining move in the Renaissance period, when the Church and Papal supremacy was defied and the Bible was brought to the common man. The Renaissance spread across Europe to Germany, England, France, and Spain from Italy from the 14th to the 16th centuries. It also laid the foundation for modern centres of learning and encouraged scientific thought.

238 **Al-Ashraf Saif al-Din Abu al-Nasr Qa'tbay was a slave under the Mamluk Sultan Barsbay.** He quickly rose through the ranks of palace guard to become the Sultan of Cairo. His reign is best remembered for the growth in commercial buildings, bridges, mosques and canals in Cairo and Alexandria. The Mamluk decorative arts included enamelled and glided glass, woodwork and inlaid metalwork.

Citadel of Qa'tbay, Alexandria, Egypt.

HISTORY OF ART AND CULTURE

239 **Sandro Botticelli was one of the foremost artists of the Renaissance.** One of his most famous paintings was the 'Adoration of the Magi' (1475 CE). Apart from its religious importance, the painting portrays some important members of Florentine society of that time, including members of the powerful Medici family. The kneeling Magi in black is, in fact, a depiction of Cosimo the Elder, founder of the Medici dynasty.

240 **Fra Filippo Lippi from Florence painted several beautiful religious pieces.** His famous altar pieces include 'Madonna and Child' and 'The Virgin and Child between SS. Frediano and Augustin'. Though he faced many scandals and lawsuits in his personal life, his fame as an artist spread mainly due to his fresco style paintings in Prato and Spoleto.

241 **The Yoruba was the greatest kingdom of present day Nigeria and Benin, from the 12th to 14th century CE.** Ife was a sacred city for these people. The Ife artists had developed a refined and naturalistic sculptural tradition using stone, brass, copper and terracotta which is unique to the artisans of Africa. The Yoruba myths believed that Ife was the centre of creation of the world and mankind.

242 **Yoruba bronze sculptures were made by artisans using a specialised technique involving clay and beeswax to create the models.** Liquid bronze was poured on top of the moulds using tubes. Once it had cooled and hardened, the clay layer was broken and the sculpture was ready! This technique was known as the 'lost wax' technique and was used to create sculptures of kings and gods of the era.

ART AND CULTURE

243 Leonardo da Vinci is considered to be the greatest Italian painter, sculptor, architect, draftsman and engineer of the Renaissance period. His paintings such as 'The Last Supper' and 'Mona Lisa' are world renowned. Among his papers, notes were found that depicted a perfect blend of artist's imagination, scientific thinking and mechanical inventiveness. He even drew the structure of a flying machine!

244 International Gothic style describes the transition of styles across Italy and Northern Europe in the interim period between Byzantine Art, Late Gothic Art and Early Renaissance Art (late 14th–early 15th century CE). The art style was elegant and decorative with special attention to details and comprised miniatures, manuscripts and ornate religious depictions. The artwork had natural and sensual figures composed within a flattened pictorial space.

245 Michelangelo was one of the foremost Renaissance artists. His most famous work was the ceiling of the Sistine Chapel in Vatican City. The majestic ceiling frescoes were created very early in his career under the commission of Pope Julius II. He spent seven years of his life (1505-1512) creating this grand work of art and was so miserable that he wrote a poem about his misery! He was also a great sculptor, and created very lifelike statues, such as the statue of David, and the Pieta.

246 **Mannerism (1520-1580) was an art style that evolved towards the end of High Renaissance in Florence and Rome.** It developed as a reaction to harmonious classicism and idealised the naturalism of High Renaissance art. Style and technique in the composition became more important than the meaning of the subject. Rosso Fiorentino and Jacopo da Pontormo were two notable artists of this period.

247 One of the most famous pieces of art from Africa during the 14th and 16th century CE was the Benin Plaque, or the 'Equestrian Oba and Attendants'. It is a brass plaque showing the King of Benin and his attendants. The distinctive coral beaded regalia and details of attendants holding shields over the Oba's head reveal a lot about the practices of the time. The varying figure sizes denote the court hierarchy. Most importantly, the beautiful detailing and skill of the piece show the high technical ability of the artists of the region.

248 **Around 1387-89, the Count of Foix wrote a treatise on hunting.** He was also known as Phoebus, and thus, his book came to be known by the same name. There are currently about 46 manuscripts of this work that have survived. Of these, the most lavishly decorated manuscripts were created in Paris in 1407. This has several famous illustrations, has the 'Hunt of the Unicorn Annunciation'.

ART AND CULTURE

249 The Quwwat-ul-Islam Mosque was built by Qutub din Aibak when he reached Delhi in 1192. He was a general of Muhammad Ghori's army. When the troops defeated Prithviraj Chauhan in the battle of Tarain, they marched to the capital, Delhi. Here, they decided to build a mosque in which to pray.

254 Later, a tower was constructed at the south-east corner of the mosque, known as the Qutub Minar. Later, rulers also expanded the mosque when the Muslim population of Delhi grew.

251 The Great Mosque of Isfahan in Iran is a classic example of congregational mosques that were and remain an important part of Muslim cities. The Great Mosque represents the genius and elegance of architecture and design of the Persian Empire that grew from the eighth century onwards. It has numerous entrances that formed a pedestrian hub. Even more than a sacred monument, it depicts a centre for commercial activities.

HISTORY OF ART AND CULTURE

252 **Ibn Battuta (1304-1368 CE) was a traveller and explorer from Morocco.** His book, *Rihla*, gives an account of his travels across many countries, including India, and his voyages thereafter by sea to China, Maldives and Java. His books give a lot of insights on the culture, botany and geography of India, southern Russia and Africa, and marks the beginning of the tradition of travel writing.

253 **Under the Vijayanagar rulers (1336-1646 CE) of Andhra Pradesh in India, many beautiful works of art were commissioned.** One of the most beautiful examples of stone carving is seen in the monumental bull near the Veerbhadra temple at Lepakshi. The statue is made of a single block of granite, and is 4.5 m high, and 8.3 m long.

250 **The 'Dasara' or Dussehra Festivities of Mysore were initiated by the Vijayanagar rulers in the 15th century CE, and continued by the later rulers.** The king and his wife would conduct the ceremony at the 'durbar' (royal court). Even today, on the ninth day of the festival, a procession is carried out in which the royal sword is worshipped and all the other weapons are carried by elephants, camels and horses.

ART AND CULTURE

255 The Inca 'Gold Llama' is a small statuette of roughly six centimetres, made completely from gold. It was excavated from the Inca tombs during excavations in Machu Pichu, Peru, and is dated back to roughly 1500 CE. This figurine was probably used by the Incan priests for rituals. The Incans used limited tools for metalwork They mainly used charcoal and flat stones as anvils, and copper pieces as hammers.

256 'The School of Athens' is a very famous fresco painted by the Renaissance artist Raphael between 1509-1511 CE. It was commissioned by Pope Julius II. In its figures, Raphael painted the likenesses of several Greek philosophers. Aristotle and Plato receive the place of honour in the centre of the painting as prominent thinkers of Western civilisation. Other important figures include Pythagoras, Ptolemy, Copernicus and Kepler.

257 Christine de Pizan, the first professional female writer, historian, moralist and poet is renowned for the publication of her book of poetry, *La Cité des Dames* in 1405. She wrote the allegorical poem questioning masculine traditions and defending women's authority. Some of the issues addressed in the book such as rape, women's access to knowledge and gender equality are relevant even today.

HISTORY OF ART AND CULTURE

258 Jean Hey (1475-1505 CE) was a painter from Netherlands. She is believed to be the mysterious artist previously known as 'Master of Moulins'. Historians believe that Hey may have been a child prodigy, having painted the famous painting of Margaret of Austria when she was just 15 years of age.

259 Jean Clouet (1480-1541 CE) was originally from the Netherlands, and was a central figure in establishing the art of portrait painting in Renaissance France. He is credited with painting King Francis I and was appointed groom of the chamber, enjoying a salary and high social position that was bestowed upon prominent poets and scholars of the time. His portrait of Guillaume Budé enabled historians to establish Clouet's style and recognise his work.

260 Tara is a female Bodhisattava in Mahayana Buddhism. She is especially popular in Tibetan iconography. The earliest representation of Tara lies in the seventh century CE Ellora caves in Maharashtra. One of the most beautiful representations of Tara as the Saviour was found in a gilt copper alloy figurine inlaid with semi-precious stones. This figurine is dated to the 14th century CE, and represents the Nepalese art of the Himalayan region.

EMPERORS, KINGS AND LEADERS

Famous Rulers

261 **James IV (1473-1513 CE) ruled Scotland from 1488 to 1513.** The young prince was just 15 when he ascended the throne, following the death of his father James III. He proved to be a wise ruler, and established good diplomatic ties with England for most of his life. However, he died in the Battle of Flodden in 1513, when the English invaded Scotland.

262 **Mehmed 1 or Mehmed Celebi was the Ottoman Sultan from 1413 to 1421.** He is known for bringing Anatolia and European territories under his control resulting in the reunification of the Ottoman Empire.

263 **Zahir-ud-din Babar (1483-1530 CE) established the Mughal Dynasty in India after defeating Ibrahim Lodi in the First Battle of Panipat in the year 1526.** Babar admired nature, so wherever he went, he built gardens. The first thing he did after taking over Delhi was to build a garden by the Yamuna River, popularly called 'Aram Bagh'.

FAMOUS RULERS

264 Ivan Vasilyevich ruled over Russia from 1533 to 1547. He was popularly called 'Ivan the Terrible' because he was ruthless, ill-tempered and terrified his subjects. It is said that he gouged out the eyes of those who constructed St. Basil's Cathedral, because he did not want another such monument to be built ever again.

265 Sigismund I (1467-1548 CE) belonged to the Jagiellon Dynasty and ruled Poland from 1506 to 1548. Sigismund and his wife were great patrons of Renaissance arts and promoted its development in Poland. Though a devout Catholic, he was secular too. He gave royal protection to Jews and allowed Greek Orthodox Christians to flourish.

266 Charles V (1500-1558 CE) ruled the Spanish Empire, the Holy Roman Empire and the Habsburg Netherlands in the early 16th century. Charles V had many enemies and was always at war. By age 56, he gave up all his kingdoms and spent the last two years of his life in a monastery.

EMPERORS, KINGS AND LEADERS

267 Sigismund II Augustus was the King of Poland and Grand Duke of Lithuania from 1548 to 1572. During his rule, there were constant troubles in his kingdom, with the nobility holding most of the power. For 20 years, he mediated between the Catholic Church and the Protestants. He also united Poland and Lithuania into the Polish-Lithuanian Commonwealth.

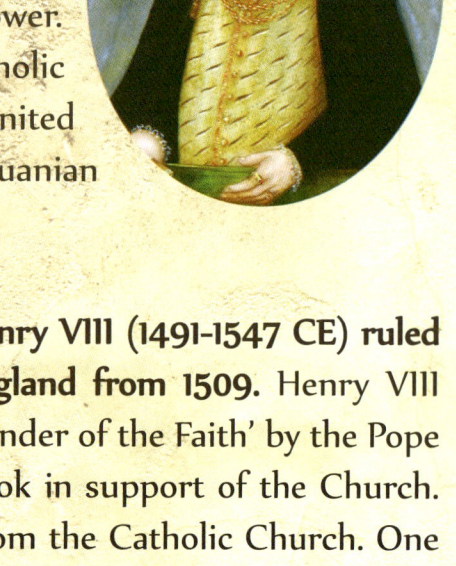

268 King Henry VIII (1491-1547 CE) ruled over England from 1509. Henry VIII was given the title 'Defender of the Faith' by the Pope because he wrote a book in support of the Church. He later broke away from the Catholic Church. One of the reasons was for this break was that he wanted divorce from his wife, Catherine of Aragon, which was not allowed by the Church. Thus, he established the Anglican Church. Henry VIII had a total of six wives.

269 Mary, Queen of Scots (1542-1587 CE) was only six days old when she succeeded her father to the throne of Scotland after his death. She was married to the French King from 1558-1560, but on his death returned to Scotland. She was considered a rival of Elizabeth I for the throne of England. She was ultimately executed by Queen Elizabeth I.

FAMOUS RULERS

270 **Francis I (1494-1547 CE) became the King of France at the age of 20.** His rivalry with Charles V led to 27 years of war, between France and England. During his reign, there were constant rifts between the Catholics and Protestants. He was given the nickname 'Francis of the Big Nose' because of his long nose.

271 **Jalal-ud-din Akbar (1542-1605 CE) is considered to be the greatest Mughal Emperor of Mughal Dynasty that ruled in India.** He ascended the throne at the age of 14. He is well-known for his love of arts and policy of religious tolerance. Akbar is famous for having assembled the Navratnas or the 'Nine Gems' in his court, who were the foremost poets, musicians, artists and generals.

272 **Mary I (1516-1558 CE) was the Queen of England and Ireland for almost five years before her death.** She wanted to bring Roman Catholicism back into England after her father Henry VIII had established the Anglican Church. She executed hundreds of Protestant leaders, which earned her the nickname 'Bloody Mary'.

EMPERORS, KINGS AND LEADERS

273 Shah Abbas I (1571-1629 CE) of the Safavid Dynasty was the Shah of Persia from 1588 till his death. During his reign, carpet weaving became a major industry, and the fame of Persian carpets spread far and wide. Abbas did not trust his family, and blinded and imprisoned his father, brothers and two sons. He even executed one of his sons. His actions left him with no heirs.

274 Henry IV (1553-1610 CE) was the first King of England from the Bourbon House. He converted to Roman Catholicism and tried to unite and bring prosperity to his kingdom after years of religious wars. There were many attempts to kill him, and he was finally murdered by a Catholic monk.

275 Michael Romanov (1596-1645 CE) was crowned the Tsar of Russia when he was just 16 years old. He founded the Romanov Dynasty and his rule marked the end of internal troubles in Russia. The famous 'Ivan Susanin' legend dramatised by Russian composer Mikhail Glinka is set in the times when Michael ruled Russia.

FAMOUS RULERS

276 Elizabeth I (1533-1603 CE) was known as the Virgin Queen. She is known as one of the greatest rulers of England. She saved England from the invasion of the Spanish Armada (fleet of ships). She brought back Protestantism to England and removed the Pope as head of the English Church. It was during her reign that Shakespeare wrote his famous plays.

277 Charles I (1600-1649 CE) ruled Great Britain and Ireland from 1625 to 1649. He had many quarrels with the Parliament of England as he believed kings were given the right to rule by god. He was finally tried in court and executed for betrayal. He was, however, a learned and knowledgeable man with a fine collection of art.

278 Gustavus II Adolf (1594-1632 CE), also known as the 'Lion of the North', reigned over Sweden from 1611 to 1632. He is said to have made Sweden a major European power, displaying his skill in military tactics. Gustavus was nearsighted and died in battle, though his troops won.

EMPERORS, KINGS AND LEADERS

279 **Tokugawa Ieyasu (1543-1616 CE) founded the Tokugawa Dynasty of Shoguns or hereditary military rulers in Japan.** Ieyasu gained supreme power in Japan by defeating the Western Army in the Battle of Sekigahara. Under Ieyasu's control, Japan remained united. He encouraged trade with foreign countries. His mausoleum at Nikko is an important shrine in Japan.

280 **Louis XIV (1638-1715 CE) was called the 'Sun King'.** He ruled France for more than 72 years, and is the longest serving monarch in European history. He built the famous Palace of Versailles. He wanted Catholicism to be the only faith in his country. The state of Louisiana in USA was named in his honour.

281 **Charles II (1630-1685 CE) was the King of England, Scotland and Ireland from 1660 onwards, and was popularly known as the 'Merry Monarch'.** His reign marked the Restoration period in English history and saw the rise of trade and colonisation in India and the US. He converted to Catholicism on his death bed.

FAMOUS RULERS

282 **Shunzhi (1638-1661 CE) was the third emperor of the Qing (Manchu) Dynasty of China, having ascended the throne at the age of six.** The emperor was a kind man and encouraged more Chinese to serve as officials in his government. The emperor was deeply influenced by Zen Buddhism.

283 **Ibrahim the Mad (1615-1648 CE) became Sultan of the Ottoman Empire in 1640.** For most of his life, until he came to the throne, he and his siblings were confined to a building within the Ottoman palace known as the Kafes, or 'cage'. It was a large building without windows, and was used as a sort of house arrest. He later suffered from frequent headaches and illnesses.

284 **Peter the Great (1672-1725 CE) was one of the most beloved rulers of Russia.** He was also known as the Tsar Reformer. He was the founder of the city of St. Petersburg. He led a major cultural revolution in Russia during his reign. He introduced the Julian calendar and the custom of decorating Christmas trees.

EMPERORS, KINGS AND LEADERS

285 James II (1633-1701 CE) was a Stuart king of England, Scotland and Ireland from 1685 to 1688. He was overthrown by William III in the 'Glorious Revolution'. He wanted to give equal rights to both the Roman Catholic and Protestant subjects. He had to abdicate his throne and flee abroad, after his army and navy deserted him.

286 William III (1650-1702 CE) was known as William of Orange. He was crowned joint monarch of England, along with his wife Mary, daughter of James II. Popularly known as King Billy, his victory in the Battle of Boyne is celebrated even today in Northern Ireland on July 12. He tried to spread the Protestant faith. He founded the Bank of England.

287 Sigismund III Vasa (1566-1632 CE) was the king of Poland and Grand Duke of Lithuania. He wanted to unite Poland and Sweden permanently. However, he ended up increasing hostilities between the two states. Sigismund III Vasa appears in a famous painting by Jan Matejko which depicts Piotr Skarga, a Polish Jesuit, preaching.

FAMOUS RULERS

288 **Wadyslaw IV Vasa (1595-1648 CE) was the successor of Sigismund III Vasa. He was a popular king who ruled Poland from 1632.** At the age of 15, he was elected Tsar of Russia, but did not keep the title as his own father was against it. As the King of Poland, he proved to be an able military man and a tolerant ruler.

289 **Leopold I (1640-1705 CE) was the Holy Roman Emperor from 1658 till his death.** Though he had studied to join the Church, he ruled over Hungary, Croatia and Bohemia. Louis XIV of France was his first cousin and his biggest rival. He was a lover of books and encouraged learning in his court.

290 **Charles XII (1682-1718 CE) became the King of Sweden in 1697, when he was 15 years old.** He was a great warrior and led Sweden in the Northern War. However, he failed in his invasion of Russia and the Swedish army became considerably weakened.

NEW LANDS

The Explorers

291 **Sir Walter Raleigh was born in East Budleigh, United Kingdom.** He was not only an adventurer and an explorer but was also a very fine writer. He was favoured by Queen Elizabeth I and was knighted in 1585.

292 **Raleigh tried to establish a colony between 1584 and 1588 near Roanoke Island that is in the present day North Carolina, USA.** He named the area 'Virginia' but never went to the place himself. He sent Captains Philip Amadas and Arthur Barlowe to explore the land in 1584.

293 **Amadas and Barlowe returned to England after a two-month exploration of the North Carolina coast in 1584.** They came back with two Native Americans, named Manteo and Wanchese. They also carried home some samples of tobacco and potatoes. They gave descriptions of the friendly inhabitants of the region and its lushness and fertility, and prompted Raleigh to attempt colonisation.

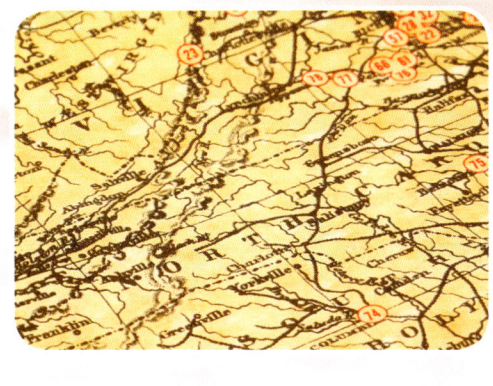

THE EXPLORERS

294 Raleigh led an expedition in 1595 to the place that is now known as Venezuela in South America. He had heard stories about the existence of 'El Dorado', which means the 'city of gold', present in the interior of South America. He located a few gold mines, but his project of colonisation was not supported at the time.

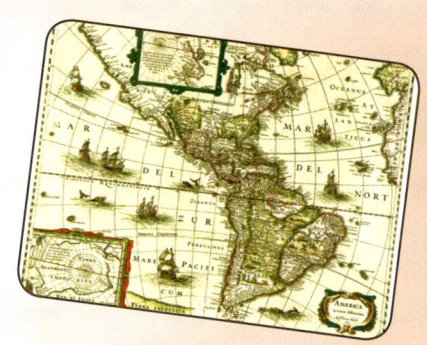

295 Raleigh, along with some other people, was accused of plotting to dethrone King James I, who was the successor of Queen Elizabeth I, and was sentenced to death. His sentence was later cancelled and instead, he was imprisoned in the Tower of London. He was released in 1616, but was not pardoned.

296 Raleigh wanted to explore the city of gold once again and, with the permission of the king, he led a second expedition to Venezuela. His son also joined him in the quest, but unfortunately died during the expedition. King James I was furious when he came to know that they had not found any trace of gold. Hence, Raleigh was executed in 1618.

NEW LANDS

297 Samuel Champlain (1574-1635 CE) was born as a French commoner who took part in the expedition to the West Indies and Central America. His good reputation earned him an unofficial title at the court of Henry IV and he came to be known as Samuel de Champlain.

298 There is a lake in Quebec province that empties into the St. Lawrence River, near New York, USA. Moreover, it is a boundary between Vermont and New York. The lake was visited for the first time by Champlain in 1609 and hence, was named Lake Champlain after him.

299 Champlain was mostly a subordinate in the expeditions until 1608, when he undertook one of his most ambitious projects as the leader of 32 colonists. The project was the founding of Quebec city in Canada. Though the winter in the city was severe, Champlain and eight other explorers survived, and in June were there to greet some more colonists who joined them.

THE EXPLORERS

FUR TRADE

300 The fur trade between France and the Native American tribes were enhanced in 1610, but after a year, there were heavy financial losses. Quebec's sponsors were ready to abandon the colony when Champlain persuaded Louis XIII to rethink the decision. The king appointed a Viceroy, who made Champlain the Commandant of 'New France—the name given to Canada at the time.

301 In 1613, Champlain went to Quebec to restore the fur trade that had been ruined in these years. He organised a company of French merchants who were able to finance trade and religious missions. Alongside this, Champlain carried out his own explorations as well.

302 In 1609, when Champlain went to Lake Huron, the Native American chiefs persuaded him to lead a war against the Iroquoi village to the south of Lake Ontario. However, he was wounded by the Iroquoi and had to spend the winter there, before returning to France the following year. The king reaffirmed Champlain's authority over Quebec, but debarred him from making any more personal explorations.

NEW LANDS

303 The first European to see the coast of Australia is believed to be a Dutch navigator, Willem Janszoon (1570-1630 CE). He was an explorer and governor of a fort in Java, under the Dutch East Indies. During one of his voyages in 1605-06, he saw the coast of Australia.

304 Although a Spanish explorer, Hernando de Soto, had discovered the entrance of the Mississippi River in 1541. A Canadian Louis Jolliet and a Jesuit Father, Jacques Marquette, were the first to explore and map the Mississippi River in 1673. They thought it was the Northwest Passage, but when they realised that the river led to the Gulf of Mexico, they returned to New France (Canada).

305 French explorer René-Robert Cavelier, sieur de La Salle was popularly known as Robert de La Salle. He claimed to have explored the whole of the Mississippi River and everything on the west side of it for France, during 1682. He had named the whole area after the French King, Louis XIV, as 'Louisiana'.

THE EXPLORERS

306 **Vitus Jonassen Bering from Denmark served in the Russian Navy.** In February 1725, he departed from St. Petersburg as the head of the expedition towards Okhotsk. His task was to map the new areas visited and to observe if Asia and America shared a land border. It was in August 1728, when Bering was sure that Asia and America were separated by a sea. This expedition earned him monetary rewards and a promotion to become a Captain Commander.

307 **Bering made his second expedition in 1741 towards North America.** Unfortunately, on the journey home, Bering fell ill. The company had to take refuge on an uninhabited island. He died on 19 December 1741 on that island, which was later given the name 'Bering Island' after the explorer. The Bering Sea, the Bering Strait, the Bering Glacier and the Bering Land Bridge are all named in honour of this explorer.

308 **Antoine de la Mothe Cadillac was a French explorer.** Besides being an explorer, he was also a trader of alcohol and furs in the 1680s. He held many important political positions, including the Commander in 1694 of Fort de Buade, which is now called St. Ignace, in Michigan. He discovered Fort Pontchartrain du Détroit, which is modern day Detroit, in 1701. He was also the Governor of Louisiana during 1710 to 1716.

NEW LANDS

309 **Charles Marie de la Condamine was a French explorer, mathematician, physicist and geographer.** La Condamine joined an expedition in 1735 to present day Ecuador with the aim of testing the hypothesis given by Isaac Newton, who had said that the Earth was not a perfect sphere, but bulged around the equator and was flat at the poles. He also explored and scientifically mapped the Amazon region during his travel.

310 **A Dutch explorer and merchant, Abel Janszoon Tasman, is known for his journeys while working for the Dutch East India Company.** He was the first European to sail to the islands of Van Diemen's Land, present day Tasmania, New Zealand. He also visited Tonga and is said to be the first to visit the Fiji Islands between 1642 and 1644.

311 **Pierre François-Xavier de Charlevoix was a French explorer, teacher and writer.** He was sent to explore Canada and to look for a route to the Pacific Ocean. From 1719-1729, he travelled via the St. Lawrence River area to the great lakes region and then to the Mississippi River. He has left behind some of the earliest accounts of North America.

THE EXPLORERS

312 A Spanish nobleman, Sebastián Vizcaíno, was also an explorer and a merchant. At the request of King Phillip II of Spain, Vizcaíno sailed to the coast of California in 1602. The viceroy, Conde de Monterey, had sponsored the journey and, therefore, Vizcaíno named the place 'Monterey Bay'. A bay in Mexico, overlooking the Pacific Ocean, is named Sebastián Vizcaíno Bay after the explorer.

313 Captain John Smith was an English explorer and soldier. He, along with almost a 100 people, sailed from England on 20 December 1606 and reached Virginia on 26 April 1607. The settlers established 'Jamestown' on 14 May 1607, which is considered to be the first permanent settlement of the English in North America.

314 Pierre-Esprit Radisson was a French explorer and fur trader. He had settled in Canada in 1651. Radisson along with his brother in law, Médard Chouart de Groseilliers, entered the English service with the formation of the Hudson's Bay Company. Both Radisson and Groseillier were the first Europeans to explore what is now Minnesota.

NEW LANDS

315 A French explorer, Jean Nicollet, was the first European to journey to the Ottawa River, down the French River, and across Lake Michigan and Green Bay, which is now called Wisconsin, in 1634. His route became a prominent fur-trading route for the French merchants.

316 Peter Minuit was born in the part of Duchy of Cleves which is now in Germany. He is well known for his purchase of the island of Manhattan from the Native Americans in 1626. He famously bought the island for about 23 dollars. He then founded New Amsterdam on the southern tip of Manhattan. Minuit also led a Swedish group in 1638 and founded New Sweden, which became the first European settlement on the Delaware River. He again bought land from Native Americans and founded Fort Christina, which is now Wilmington, Delaware in the USA.

THE EXPLORERS

317 Eusebio Francisco Kino was an Italian explorer, a Jesuit missionary and astronomer. He was also a mapmaker and a mathematician. He had explored many areas in southwestern North America which included northern Sonora (now in Mexico), southern California and southern Arizona, both of which are now in the USA.

318 Kino took part in more than 40 expeditions in 1691 where he went on to explore southern Arizona via the Rio Grande, to the Colorado River, and then the Gila River. He discovered the sources of these rivers and became the first person to map all these rivers. He even discovered that lower California was not an island but a peninsula, the Baja Peninsula.

319 Sir Henry Hudson was an English navigator and explorer. He travelled twice, in 1607 and 1608, for the sake of the English merchants to find a route to Cathay (China) from above the Arctic Circle. He even explored the Hudson River, which has been given his name. Hudson's Bay Company was named after him.

320 A Dutch explorer, Dirck Hartog, was the first European to write accounts of the western coast of Australia. Hartog began his sailing from Amsterdam and had to stop at the Cape of Good Hope due to a storm. It was on 25 October 1616 that he came upon some uninhabited islands. He landed on one of them. This island was later named Dirk Hartog Island after him.

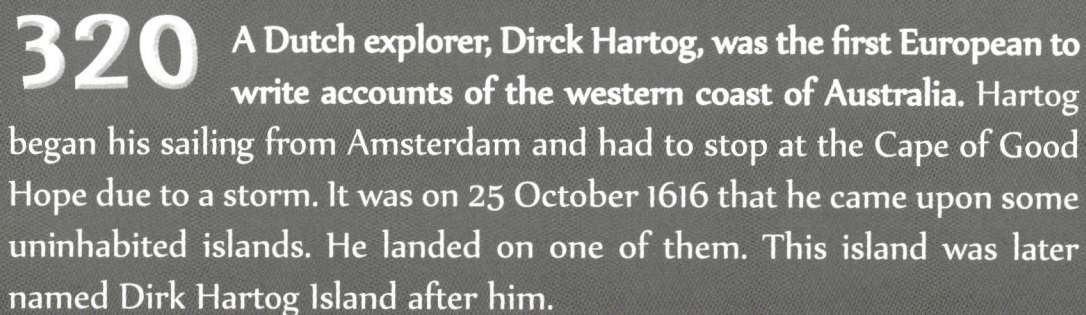

CHANGING WORLD

The Industrial Revolution

321 Although the Industrial Revolution is dated to about 1760, its beginnings can be traced back more than 200 years before this. Inventors and scientists such as Descartes, Bacon and Galileo had already made important discoveries and come up with unique ideas that ultimately led to in the Industrial Revolution.

322 The Industrial Revolution happened in two phases, from 1760 to the years 1820-40. This was the time of modern inventions, that led to a massive increase in production. The machines that were invented during the time of the Industrial Revolution could perform the tasks and jobs that were earlier done manually or with the help of domesticated animals.

323 The first country where the Industrial Revolution started was Great Britain. From there, it later spread across Europe, North America and other countries around the globe.

THE INDUSTRIAL REVOLUTION

324 Industrial Revolution is said to have been born and promoted by the British because of two major reasons. First, Great Britain was a country that had abundant resources of iron ore and coal that were required to power the machines needed for industrialisation. Second, it was a very stable country, both politically and economically.

325 Britain was a leading colonial power at this time, and its colonies supplied raw materials at low cost for producing the goods. They also provided a marketplace for selling the manufactured goods.

326 The Industrial Revolution caused a major shift in the population of London, as people started moving from the rural countryside to the cities. Between 1801 and 1871, London witnessed a boom in population, which rose from 939,000 to 3,244,000

CHANGING WORLD

327 The Industrial Revolution can also be termed as an 'Economic Revolution' as it changed the way countries manufactured goods. Countries that were largely agricultural now turned into industrial hubs. People started leaving their land in search of better livelihood in the cities. However, most of these people were forced to live in poverty in the cities.

328 The most notable advancement in technology during this time was the invention of steam-powered rail engines, using coal and petroleum as fuels to heat water and turn it into steam. This led to a revolution in industries, such as manufacturing and textiles.

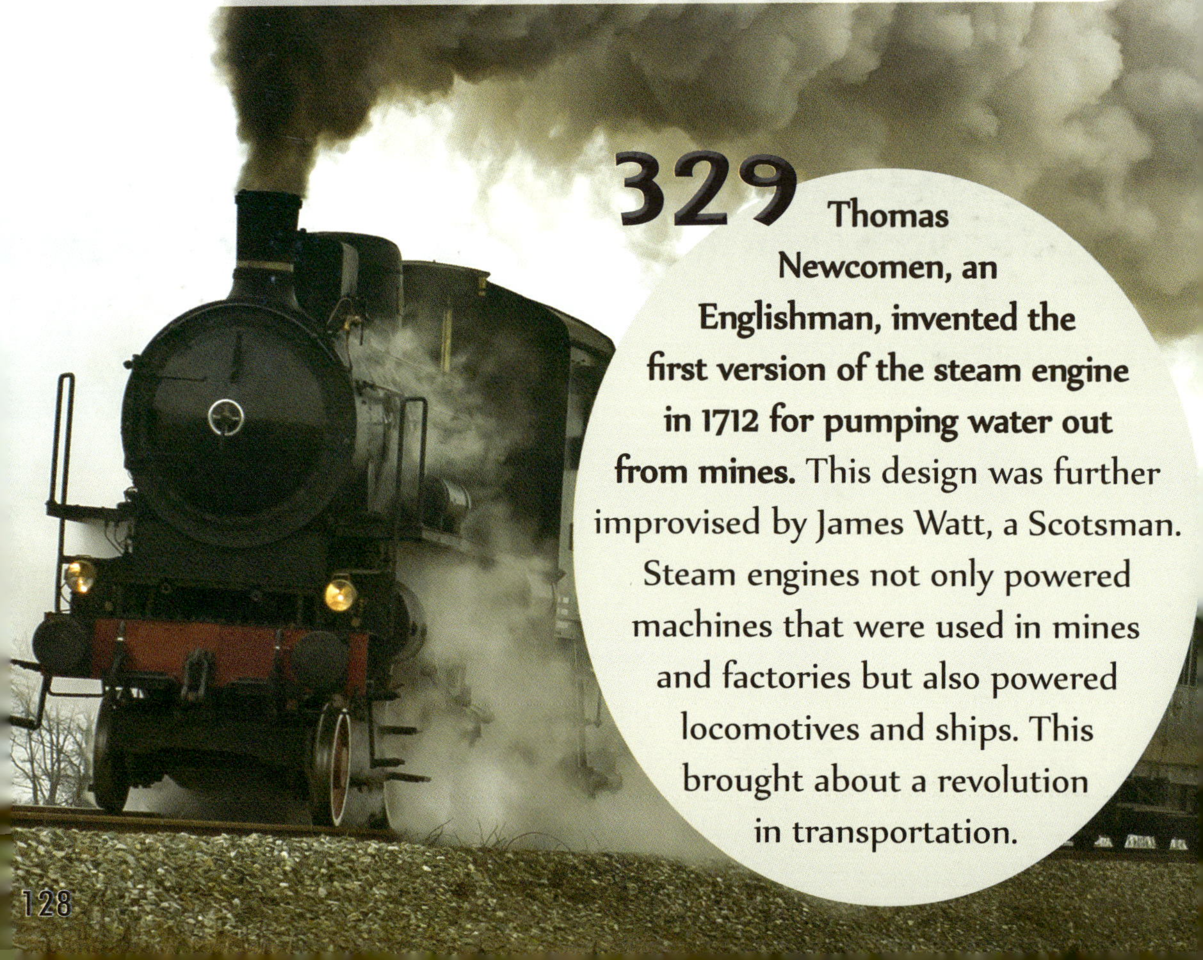

329 Thomas Newcomen, an Englishman, invented the first version of the steam engine in 1712 for pumping water out from mines. This design was further improvised by James Watt, a Scotsman. Steam engines not only powered machines that were used in mines and factories but also powered locomotives and ships. This brought about a revolution in transportation.

THE INDUSTRIAL REVOLUTION

330 This period also witnessed great technological advancement. One of the most significant inventions was the 'assembly line' by Henry Ford. Other important inventions that prepared Great Britain for the revolution were the spinning jenny by James Hargreaves (1764), the water frame by Richard Arkwright (1769) and the spinning mule by Samuel Crompton (1779).

331 The invention and advancement of the telegraph in the 1830s and 1840s made communication swift and easy. Messages could be sent and received immediately, as opposed to letters that took weeks to reach overseas.

332 Despite the marked changes and prosperity the Industrial Revolution brought, it has been largely held responsible for the steep rise in pollution in our planet. Industries were thriving, but they were also releasing massive amounts of poisonous gases into the atmosphere, and toxic waste on to land and water.

CHANGING WORLD

333 Natural resources such as coal and petroleum were needed to fuel the industries and therefore these non-renewable resources were consumed at an alarming rate.

334 The economic conditions did improve during the Industrial Revolution, but there was also a growing number of poor people from the working classes who were faced with long working hours, dangerous jobs and subhuman living conditions. The dissatisfaction amongst these people often led to rioting, protests and social breakdowns.

335 Before the Industrial Revolution, a majority of the factories were powered with the help of water. Hence, they had to be located near the river as waterwheels provided them with power to run the machines.

The ancient waterwheels in Hama Syria.

THE INDUSTRIAL REVOLUTION

336 **During the Industrial Revolution, the steam-powered printing press was devised.** It made it easier and quicker to print books and newspapers. Mass printing made these papers cheaper than before and more accessible to people, who were now eager to read the news. It thus led to an increase in literacy.

337 Manchester in England became the hub of the textile industry and was fondly called 'Cottonopolis' during the Industrial Revolution.

338 Around 1811-16, a group of weavers started protesting against large factories, as their traditional livelihood was being stolen. They destroyed machinery and went on riots. Such people were known as 'Luddites', after the name of their leader, Ned Ludd.

CHANGING WORLD

339 Although most countries have undergone the Industrial Revolution sooner or later, there are still some countries in Asia and Africa that are said to have not experienced it completely. Such countries are often called 'Developing or Third World Countries'.

340 The Industrial Revolution gave rise to 'Capitalism', a new economic system based on the most efficient means of production. Capitalism placed more importance on producing profits on the initial amount of capital invested into any industry. The rise of capitalism later laid the ground for international trading.

341 The Industrial Revolution began in the northeast part of the USA in the New England area. A lot of historians credit the beginning of the revolution in the US to the launch of the Slater's Mill in Massachusetts in 1793. Samuel Slater was raised in England and gained a good understanding of textile mills, before he put it into practice in the United States.

THE INDUSTRIAL REVOLUTION

342 Towards the end of the 18th century, the United States was the world's most industrialised country. However, at the same time, other British colonies, such as India had been completely de-industrialised. For instance, India which was previously one of the world's top producers of high quality cotton textile was now forced into only providing raw materials and buying British textiles.

343 The Industrial Revolution was a little delayed in Europe and began a few years after it came to Britain. Many European industries thus had the benefit of improving upon the technology that had already been evolved in Britain. Often, the technology was brought along by the British entrepreneurs and engineers who moved to different European countries in search of fresh opportunities.

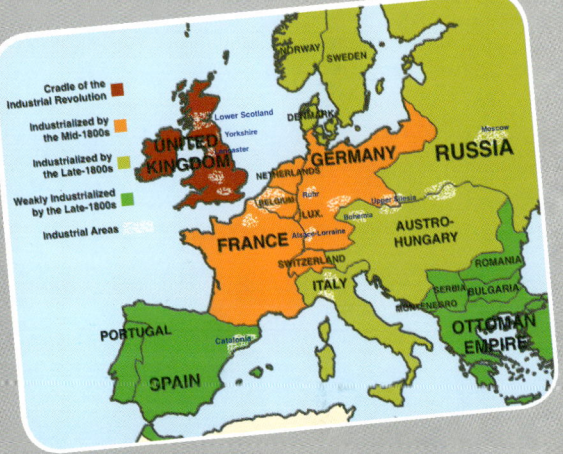

344 'Miniature England' is a term coined for the Ruhr Valley in Wesphalia (now modern-day Germany), which in 1809 looked quite similar to the industrial regions of England.

CHANGING WORLD

345 In France, the Industrial Revolution followed its own course, which was different from what had been seen in other countries. The French industrialisation route was slow but consistent throughout the 18th and 19th centuries. French industrialisation commenced around 1815 but only lasted till 1860. This was followed by an economic crisis between 1860 and 1905. Thereafter, industrialisation picked pace after 1905.

346 The US offered important technological advancements during the Industrial Revolution in the form of the cotton gin, development of machine tools, and a process of manufacturing interchangeable parts. This catapulted the US as the most industrialised country of the world during the later part of the 19th century.

347 In Japan, the Industrial Revolution commenced around 1870, as the leaders of the Meiji era wanted to be at par with the West. Railroads, roads and land reform programmes were launched to support overall development.

THE INDUSTRIAL REVOLUTION

348 The Japanese also initiated a new education system for their students, based on the Western education system. They recruited over 3,000 Western teachers, while sending thousands of their students to the West to gain knowledge.

349 Japanese politicians toured the United States and Europe as part of the 'Iwakura Mission' to gain more knowledge about the western way of doing things. Industrialisation became a state policy and the Bank of Japan utilised taxes for funding textile and steel factories.

350 The Japanese Industrial Revolution saw the growth and enhancement of its textile-related industries, such as cotton and silk.

Histories of the Continents

351 One of the longest lasting ancient civilisations was the Egyptian civilisation. It survived for more than 3,000 years. We know a lot about the ancient Egyptians and their way of life through the structures that they built, such as the Pyramids, their paintings, and their writings in the hieroglyphic script. Did you know that the famous Egyptian queen, Cleopatra, was actually from Macedonia in northern Greece?

The Pyramids of Giza are the only one of the seven ancient wonders that is still intact.

352 Vasco da Gama was an explorer from Portugal who became famous for discovering the sea route from Europe to India in 1497-99. He travelled around the southernmost tip of Africa, known as the Cape of Good Hope. His route to India was a significant discovery and led to improved trade between the East and West and eventual rise of colonisation in Asia.

HISTORIES OF THE CONTINENTS

353 World War I started on the 28 July 1914 and ended on 11 November 1918. Although the war was concentrated in Europe, it was considered a war on a global scale. The warring countries were split into two alliances at the time. The war was fought between the Allies and the Central Alliance. The trigger of the war was the assassination of the Archduke of Austria-Hungary. However, each country had its own reasons for joining the war. Most of the European countries at the time were trying to win back territories they had lost during previous wars.

354 World War II was a global war that started in 1939 and ended in 1945. It involved most countries of the world. Again, two alliances were created: the Axis and the Allies. This war was the deadliest war seen so far, and resulted in more than 75 million deaths. It eventually ended after the invasion of Germany by the Western Allies and the Soviet Union. Japan, one of the Axis powers, surrendered after the United States destroyed the cities of Hiroshima and Nagasaki with atom bombs in August 1945.

CHANGING WORLD

355 The Holocaust is associated with some of the most horrific memories of World War II that were inflicted by the Nazis in Germany. This was a mass murder of nearly 6 million Jews that was sponsored by the state. Adolf Hitler, leader of the Nazi Party in Germany, ordered his army to imprison and kill Jews in facilities, such as concentration camps, work camps and extermination camps. By the end of the war, nearly 2/3rd of the Jewish population had been massacred.

356 The Vietnam War took place between North and South Vietnam and lasted for over 18 years, starting on 1 November 1955 and ending on 30 April 1975. While North Vietnam received support from the Viet Cong, the Soviet Union, China and other communist ally countries, South Vietnam received support from the United States of America and other anti-communist ally nations. In Vietnam, this war is known as the 'Resistance War' against the US. In the year 1973, the US Congress ended the involvement of their military in Vietnam by passing the Case-Church Amendment. This resulted in the war finally ending in 1975.

357 **The Seven Years' War was fought between France and Britain in North America between 1756 and 1763.** The two countries were competing against each other to colonise the newly discovered continent, and were trying to gain control over as many areas as each could. However, the British declared war when they realised that France had enhanced its occupation well into the Ohio River, and posed a threat to their plans. The war between France and Britain extended to other colonies, such as in India. Eventually, the war was brought to an end in 1763 with the signing of the Treaty of Paris, according to which Britain was given the right to retain Canada as its colony.

358 **The ancient Roman city of Pompeii is located near Naples, Italy.** On 24 August, 79 CE, Pompeii was destroyed by the eruption of Mount Vesuvius. The eruption buried the city under a 20 feet layer of ash and molten lava. Nearly 16,000 people perished. Pompeii was first found in 1599, but was explored in greater detail only in 1748. Today, it is a UNESCO World Heritage Site, and has been a popular tourist destination for over 250 years now.

CHANGING WORLD

359 Chernobyl is a Ukrainian town which saw a devastating nuclear accident on 26 April 1986. The nuclear disaster happened due to a power surge in reactor while conducting a systems test, which led to an explosion and fire that spewed radioactive chemicals into the atmosphere. Massive rescue and evacuation operations were conducted in the adjoining areas, but despite their efforts, many people died due to radiation, while the health of many was impacted.

360 The Black Plague or the Black Death, was a pandemic disease that spread throughout Europe and the Mediterranean during the 14th century and killed between 75 and 200 million people. The origin of the plague is still disputed, but it may have been transmitted to Europe from Central Asia. Another theory claims that the plague was transmitted through Mongol armies or traders across the Silk Road and had apparently killed millions of Asians before it struck Europe. The recent DNA analysis of the Black Plague shows that the bacterium responsible for the pandemic was Yersinia pestis that apparently wiped out 30-60 per cent of the European population.

HISTORIES OF THE CONTINENTS

361 **The French Revolution took place in 1789, during a time of social and political rebellion in France.** There was huge inequality between the rich and the poor. It started on 14 July 1789, when the French citizens forcefully entered the Bastille prison in Paris. The revolution lasted for nearly 10 years until 1799, and led to the downfall of the French Monarchy. Many members of the nobility were publically executed, including King Louis XVI and Marie Antoinette. The revolution also marked the beginning of the rule of Napoleon Bonaparte.

CHANGING WORLD

362 The Vikings came from Scandinavia. They were sea warriors who were most active between 800 CE and 1066 CE. They spoke the Norse language. The word 'viking' in Norse meant 'pirate raid', hence they not only traded but also invaded various countries across Europe, North Africa, the Middle East, Central Asia and the Mediterranean. The Vikings were the masters of the sea and travelled long distances. It is said that they had reached as far as Canada by 1000 CE.

363 The Silk Road was a trade route that spanned 4000 miles all the way from China to Eastern Europe, with links to Persia and India along the route. The Silk Road was first used extensively during the Han Dynasty rule in China during 207-220 BCE and continued to be important all the way into the 15th century. However, after the discovery of sea trading routes in the 16th century, the importance of the Silk Road declined. The term 'Silk Road' was coined in 1870 by Ferdinand van Richthofen, a German geographer who wanted to highlight the historical importance of this trade route.

HISTORIES OF THE CONTINENTS

364 The Reign of Terror was part of the events of the French Revolution. It refers to a 10-month time period between September 1793 and July 1794, when revolutionaries executed nearly 16,000 people by the guillotine. It is estimated that nearly 25,000 people were executed throughout France without a fair trial. Despite its slogan of 'Liberty, Equality and Fraternity', the French Revolution with its brutal executions created an environment of fear and anarchy in France.

365 The Shang Dynasty is the first Chinese Dynasty for which extensive archaeological remains have been found. Their rule began from about 1558 and continued till 1046 BCE. The Shang rule grew along the banks of the Yellow River. The river banks were fertile, but were prone to flooding. The Shang Dynasty lasted for more than five centuries, ruled by about 30 emperors.

CHANGING WORLD

366 The Samurai of Japan were early warriors, who eventually became high ranking nobles and ruled Japan from 1603-1867. Also known as 'Bushi', the Samurai followed the Bushido code of skill, bravery, honour, obedience, self sacrifice and self discipline. Each Samurai was armed with a sword and a special 'kabuto' helmet and armour. In special cases, someone from outside Japan could also become a samurai. Female samurai were known as Onna-Bugeisha.

367 The League of Nations had been set up to preserve peace after the World War 1. However, it was not effective in stopping the World War II. Therefore, at the end of the World War II, many nations suggested that the League of Nations be replaced, so as to prevent another such conflict. Thus, the United Nations was born on 24 October 1945. Its objectives included maintaining human rights, social progress, peace, humanitarian aid, environmental protection and security. It initially started off with 51 member nations, it now has 193 countries as its members.

368 **The ancient cities of Mohenjo-daro and Harappa belonged to the Indus Valley Civilisation.** The remains of Harappa were mentioned in 1842 by Charles Masson, a British traveller. In 1856, some ancient burnt bricks were discovered and were used to lay railway lines between Karachi and Lahore. It was only in the 1920s that actual archaeological excavation and study was conducted on the area. These two cities are believed to have existed 3000 BC, to 1600 BC and were quite similar in terms of their planning.

Mohenjo-daro city ruins in Pakistan.

CHANGING WORLD

369 **Christopher Columbus set out to find India in 1492.** He sailed westward, trying to find an alternate sea route to Asia. However, his expedition led him to North America instead. His discovery of America helped Europeans colonise the new continents. Explorers started coming in from countries, such as the Netherlands, France and Spain, to explore the offerings of this new country. The Spanish explorers mostly colonised the regions of South America, while France, England and the Netherlands colonised North America.

370 **The term 'Renaissance' means 'rebirth'.** It is used to refer to a time period in Europe between the 14th and 17th century. After the downfall of the Roman Empire, the Middle Ages were seen as a dark period, when a lot of the advances in government, art and science made by the Romans and Greeks were lost. The Renaissance was thus a period which revived science, art, music, literature and education.

371 **The Cold War was a long period of strain between the East European countries, led by the Soviet Union, and the Western countries, led by the United States.** At the time, the Soviet Union and the United States were known as superpowers. They did not fight an obvious, all-guns-blazing war, but indulged in proxy wars. This period was also the era of the space race and the arms race, and lasted from 1945 to 1991, ending with the disintegration of the Soviet Union.

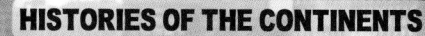

HISTORIES OF THE CONTINENTS

372 **The period of economic crisis during the 1930s is known as the Great Depression.** It started in the USA, but eventually spread to many other countries across the world. This period was marked by unemployment, poverty, homelessness and hunger. The Great Depression began in October 1929, when the stock market crashed, due to failure of banks, soaring consumer debts, volatile stock speculation, overproduction of goods and drought.

373 **Napoleon Bonaparte is known as one of the greatest French generals.** He proclaimed himself the Emperor of France from 1804-1814. He helped establish French control over a large part of the continent, including the Netherlands, Switzerland, parts of Italy and Germany. He established the Napoleonic code, which was based on the ideals of the French Revolution. Many of our modern ideas, like religious tolerance, equality before law, and meritocracy were spread by Napoleon.

CHANGING WORLD

374 **The Industrial Revolution has been seen as an outcome of the Renaissance and gave rise to scientific thought in Europe.** This led to many inventions and discoveries, which helped in the mechanisation of industries. The Scientific Revolution of this period also supported the exploration of new lands, and led to the rise of social sciences, such as anthropology, geography and history writing.

375 **'Apartheid' refers to a system of laws that were created in 1948 to segregate the South African community based on race, where the indigenous 'black' population was dominated by the Afrikaans-speaking 'white' minority.** The restrictions that came through apartheid led to resistance and this finally led to the creation of the African National Congress that led the liberation movement. Apartheid eventually ended on 27 April 1994. The most famous leader of this movement was Nelson Mandela. The end of apartheid enabled South Africans of all races to vote in a national election for the first time.

376 **Senator Barack Obama of Illinois became the first African-American President of the United States.** He was elected to power on 4 November 2008. Obama became the 44th President of the United States of America who was also elected for a second term on 6 November 2012. Obama's father was a black man from Kenya, while his mother was a white woman from the US. He went on to study at the reputed Colombia University and Harvard Law School.

HISTORIES OF THE CONTINENTS

377 'Brexit' is a term combining the words 'British and Exit' given to the United Kingdom's referendum which took place in June 2016. This was done to make a decision about whether or not Britain would continue to be part of the European Union. About 52 per cent voted in favour of leaving the EU.

378 On 1 May 2011, American troops stormed a compound in Abbottabad in Pakistan, where the most wanted terrorist and leader of the terrorist group, Al-Qaida, Osama bin Laden, was hiding. He was killed during the operation. This was an important event in the war against terrorism that the US had been waging since 2001.

CHANGING WORLD

379

Neil Alden Armstrong, a US astronaut, was the first man to walk on the moon on 21 July 1969. The words he spoke 240,000 miles away from Earth while stationed on the moon that reached billions at home and changed space exploration were: "That's one small step for man, one giant leap for mankind."

HISTORIES OF THE CONTINENTS

380 After the Russian Revolution of 1917, the country came to be known as the Union of Soviet Socialist Republics (**USSR**). The USSR developed their own space programme, and on 12 April 1961, Yuri Gagarin travelled on the spacecraft Vostok I and became the first man to enter the space. Soviet astronauts are called cosmonauts.

381 In 1905, a revolt against European domination arose in the continent of Africa. It came to be known as the Maji-Maji rebellion. At the time, a person who claimed to be a medium for spirits claimed to have a water which could render people bullet-proof. 'Maji' in Swahili means 'water'. The revolt was crushed.

382 King Leopold of Belgium ruled over Zaire in Africa with a heavy hand. His reign lasted from 1885 to 1908. He was ruthless and was responsible for wiping out half of the Zairians to gain wealth for himself.

383 A law was passed in 1913 that reserved 87 per cent of the land for the white people in South Africa. The law was called 'The Native Land Act'. It displaced many native Africans who were then forced to work for the Europeans.

The World Wars

384 On 8 January 1912, the African National Congress was formed. Their aim was to fight for the right of the African people. Pixley Seme was one of the founders of ANC.

385 In China, a secret group was formed to fight the European intrusion. They were named the 'Society of Harmonious Fists'. They earned the name 'Boxers'. The Boxer rebellion took place in 1900, where the Chinese people opposed growing attempts by the Europeans to gain power. Though the rebellion was crushed, it marked the end of outside interference in Chinese affairs at the time.

386 When the Russian ships were defeated by the Japanese at the Tsushima Strait in May 1905, it was for the first time that a European fleet was defeated by an Asian one!

THE WORLD WARS

387 **In the first century CE, the Roman army had driven off the Jewish people from Palestine, their homeland.** In the 19th century, a movement called 'Zionism' was started, to give the Jewish people their homeland back.

388 **To end their disputes, Britain and France signed a treaty called the 'Entente Cordiale' in 1904.** It was a guarantee that both the countries would not try to obstruct each other's empire building, colonising activities.

389 The 'pickelhaube' or 'pickelhelm' was the helmet worn by imperial German officers in the 19th and 20th centuries. These helmets bore a design of an eagle, which was representative of the ruling house of Prussia at that time.

CHANGING WORLD

390 **The Anglo-Russian Treaty was signed in 1907.** At the time, both nations were powerful colonisers. While Britain was expanding its control northwards from India, Russia was expanding rapidly over Central Asia. They agreed not to annex Afghanistan, which became a buffer state between the two.

391 **At the turn of the 20th century, Ireland wanted independence from British rule.** To achieve their aim, the Irish people planned a rising in Dublin. The event is known as the 'Easter Rising' because it came to fruition on the Easter Sunday in 1916.

392 **Russia was declared a republic in September 1917 by the Provisional Government.** However, in October it was declared the Soviet Union when Vladimir Lenin organised a coup and seized power. He was a member of the Bolshevik Party. Some of the popular slogans of the time were 'All power to the Soviets', and 'Peace, bread, land'. The last members of the previous ruling house, the Romanovs, were killed in 1918.

THE WORLD WARS

393 Theodore Roosevelt was elected the President of the United States from 1901 to 1909. He won a Nobel Peace Prize because of his mediation to end the Russo-Japanese War in 1905.

394 The American continent, mainly North America, saw several waves of mass immigration from the time it was colonised. One of the major waves of colonisation took place in the 1940s, when the potato famine in Ireland caused thousands to flee to North America to escape the poverty and famine in their homeland. The majority of immigrants were young people, aged between 15 and 30 years.

395 Henry Ford caused a revolution in the transport industry when he changed the production time of a car assembly from 12 hours to just about 2 hours. This brought in the era of mass produced cars. The first car model which took the world by storm was the Model T, introduced in 1908.

CHANGING WORLD

396 **Hipolito Yrigoyen, the President of Argentina in 1916, was known as the 'Father of the Poor'.** He improved working conditions for factory workers. He also refused to support either side in World War I.

397 **In 1901, the Commonwealth of Australia was established.** The government was still answerable to the British power, but now the previously divided six colonies were treated as one entity.

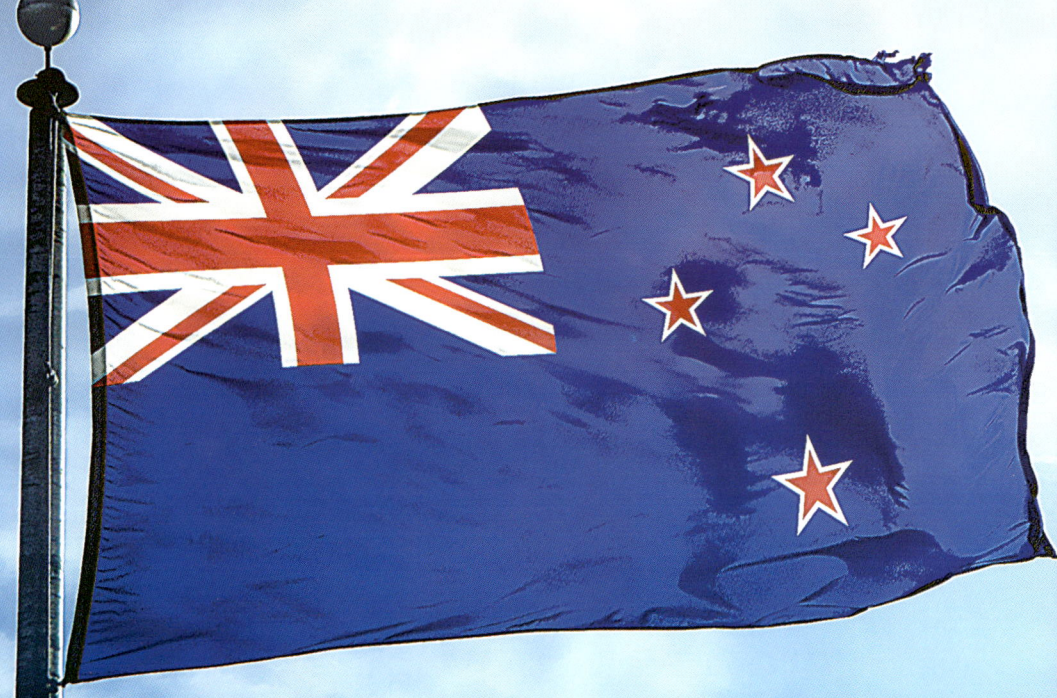

398 **New Zealand was the first country to give elder citizens the provision of getting pensions.** It also was the first nation to grant women the right to vote.

THE WORLD WARS

399 **The British arrived in Australia in the 18th century.** However, the aboriginal population had already been living on the continent for 40,000 years. The aboriginals were persecuted by the British settlers. It was only in 1967 that they were granted the status of full citizens by the government.

400 **The native people, the Maoris, were ill treated by colonialists in New Zealand.** Apirana Ngata fought for the rights of Maoris and was knighted by the British government in 1927 for his work.

401 **On 28 July 1914, Austria declared war on Serbia.** There were several treaties already in place among different European nations, maintaining a system of checks and balances. Because of this web of treaties, very soon most European nations had to join the war. The war soon spread to the colonies of the European nations as well.

CHANGING WORLD

402 Russia was defeated by Germany at Tannenberg in August 1914. This loss sustained by Russia made the common people furious. They were against the war and demanded that Russia withdraw from it. However, the Tsar did not do so, and this became one of the major reasons behind the Russian Revolution of 1917.

403 At the beginning of World War I, many people joined the army willingly. The armies used posters to urge people to fight for their country. However, soon it became mandatory for people to join the armed forces and those who resisted were imprisoned.

404 As the men joined the armies and left to fight in the World War I, it left the factories at home without workers. During this time the women stepped up and for the first time started taking on a more active role in running factories, farms, and other such important roles.

THE WORLD WARS

405 **The League of Nations was established in 1920.** Its aim was to maintain peace throughout the world in order to avoid another world war. It started out with 42 members, but by the time it was dissolved in 1946, it only had 23.

406 **In 1931, for the first time, a railway line was laid down that linked the continent of Africa from east to west.** This railway line was built by the European powers to facilitate trade and commerce.

407 **Morocco was a contested site wanted by both Spain and France.** In 1912, they agreed to share by dividing it amongst themselves. The north became a Spanish settlement and the south became a French settlement.

CHANGING WORLD

408 Did you know that native Africans had to carry passes in their own home continent in the 19th and 20th centuries? Their movements were very restricted. The system of 'apartheid' was born during this time. It is a form of racial segregation.

409 Mahatma Gandhi undertook the 'Salt March' in 1930. He did this in defiance of the British government which was levying heavy taxes on basic commodities, like salt. This peaceful protest gathered a lot of attention worldwide.

410 On 13 April 1919, British soldiers, under the command of General Reginald Dyer, opened fire on a crowd of innocent people in the Jallianwallah Bagh. This infuriated the Indian people and added to their agitation against the British rule. General Dyer was removed from active service in 1920.

THE WORLD WARS

411 As the first president of Turkey, Mustafa Kemal encouraged western education and modernisation, and was popularly known as Attaturk, or 'father' in Turkish.

412 During both the World Wars, the weather conditions were the soldiers worst enemy. They had to cross high mountains, dangerous landforms and extreme weather conditions to get to the point of attack and back home.

413 Oil became an important commodity in the 20th century. The oil mining industry boomed after the wars. Baghdad, the largest city of Iraq, which is also its capital, grew wealthy due to its oil wells.

Iraq emerged as a major oil-producing country in the 20th century.

CHANGING WORLD

414 After the end of the First World War, unemployment and inflation cast its long shadow over Europe in the 1920s. The US economy too faced its effects, though it had not participated in the war.

415 After World War 1, there was a social change in Europe. Women had taken on active roles during the war, and now started demanding more rights. Their role during the war had finally helped to get them voting rights in most countries of Europe. At the same time, women's fashion also changed, as women were spotted wearing shorter hairstyles and higher hemlines. These simpler styles showed the requirements of the new working women.

416 Motorcar manufacturing increased before and after the war. Europe followed the footsteps of the US and launched small cars such as Austins in Britain for increased mobility. At the same time, technological improvements were also carried out for military vehicles, including submarines and tanks.

THE WORLD WARS

417 President Hindenburg had made Adolf Hitler the Chancellor of Germany in 1933. When the President died in 1934, Hitler became the leader of Germany. The Nazis banned other political parties and used various mediums to impose their beliefs onto the public.

418 Hitler's aim was to rebuild the German economy. At the end of the World War 1, Germany had to cede certain mining areas to France, and also had to pay heavy war reparations to the victorious countries. One of the areas that the Germans focused on was automobiles. They wanted to make a car that every Germans could afford. This led to the development of the brand Volkswagen. Volkswagen 'Beetle' became one of the most famous cars in the world during that time.

419 In the US, during the Great Depression of 1929, many people lost their jobs and became unemployed. In the big cities, soup kitchens were established which offered free food to the poor.

CHANGING WORLD

420 To end the Great Depression in the US, Franklin D. Roosevelt who was elected as the president of the US in 1933 introduced the concept of the 'New Deal'. The focus of the initiative was to create new opportunities and end unemployment.

421 The 'talkies' in the cinema industries were also introduced during the time of the Great Depression. The first full length feature film released as a talkie was the 1927 film *The Jazz Singer*. These fictional accounts of famous characters led the masses to believe in the 'American dream'.

422 Coffee made its way to Brazil in the early 1700s and became an integral part of the economy. By 1900, Brazil was responsible for 70 per cent of the world's coffee supply!

THE WORLD WARS

423 **Australia was able to recover from the world depression faster than the other countries because of its gold reserves.** The price of gold went up in between the two world wars, and helped the country pull through.

424 **On 3 September 1939, France and Britain declared war on Germany after it invaded Poland.** Germany used weapons of destructions which were unparalleled. The system of combat they utilised was called Blitzkrieg, 'the lightning war', which proved to be very effective.

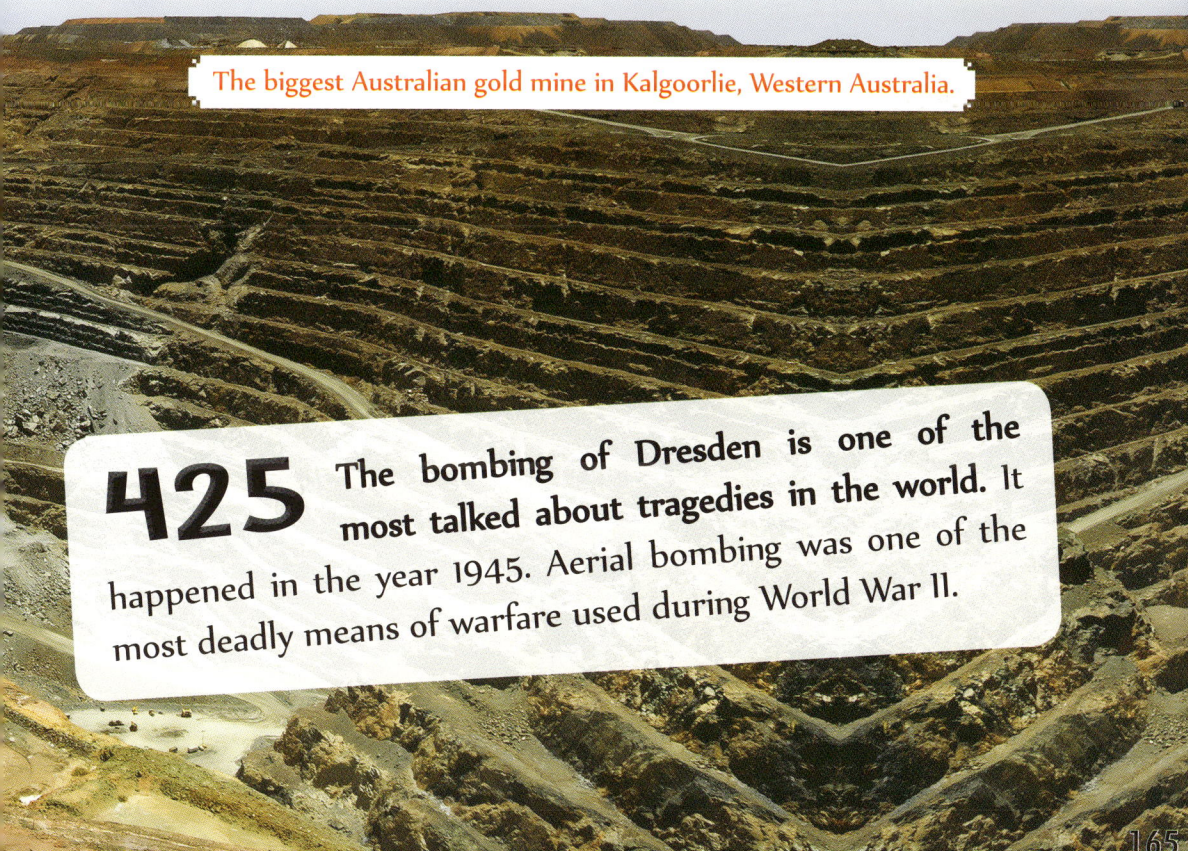

The biggest Australian gold mine in Kalgoorlie, Western Australia.

425 **The bombing of Dresden is one of the most talked about tragedies in the world.** It happened in the year 1945. Aerial bombing was one of the most deadly means of warfare used during World War II.

CHANGING WORLD

426 Before and during the World War II, Jews were terrorised by the Nazis. They were blamed for all Germany's ills, and were forced to live in a small corner of the cities. They were made to wear identity badges as well. Later, they were systematically killed. Many Jews escaped in dangerous conditions to other countries like Hungary and the US.

427 The first atomic bomb was dropped by the US on 6 August, 1945 on Hiroshima, Japan. It caused massive destruction. The second bomb was dropped on the nearby city of Nagasaki. There are memorial museums dedicated to the lives lost in the bombing in Japan. One such museum is the Hiroshima Peace Memorial Museum.

The Hiroshima Peace Memorial Museum in Hiroshima, Japan.

428 On 8 May 1945, the Prime Minister of Britain, Winston Churchill, officially declared it to be the 'Victory in Europe Day'. This marked the end of World War II in the continent. Before this, on 30 April, Hitler had committed suicide. On 7 May, the Germans officially signed the document of surrender.

THE WORLD WARS

429 On 24 October 1945, the United Nations was formally established. It had 51 founder states. The number is now 193. As more and more countries were freed from colonial rule, they joined the organisation.

430 **World War II is said to have claimed 50 million lives.** Many people lost their homes and employment. Once again, women played a major role in maintaining the daily lives of the warring nations while the men went to war.

EXPANDING WORLD

A Global Outreach

431 After the atomic bombing of Japan put an end to World War II, the world hoped for an end to war. In fact, World War II was known as the 'War to end all wars', because people were sure that no one wanted to see such carnage again. However, the USA and the USSR were engaged in a silent tussle for power known as the Cold War. There was suspicion on both sides and they continued to build up their weaponry.

Statue of Kwame Nkrumah at Kwame Nkrumah Memorial Park in Accra, Ghana.

432 Ghana's movement for independence was led by Kwame Nkrumah (1909-1972). He had a vision for a united Africa and was a huge inspiration for many people.

A GLOBAL OUTREACH

433 After the end of World War II, Libya was the first African country to gain independence in 1951. One by one, the other countries of the continent gained independence from the European powers by 1968.

434 In February 1990, Nelson Mandela was released from jail after serving 27 years as a political prisoner. He played a leading role in the fight against apartheid and was awarded the Nobel Peace Prize in 1993.

435 After World War II, the British Empire lost hold of its Asian colonies. In 1947, India got its independence. The country was divided into two nations—India and Pakistan. Later, in 1971, Pakistan further split into two, creating Bangladesh.

436 Korea was divided into North Korea and South Korea in the year 1945. The North was a communist state under Soviet influence, while the South was a capitalist state aided by the USA. In 1950, North Korea invaded the South, leading to war that lasted till 1953.

EXPANDING WORLD

437 The Japanese economy started improving after years of war torn depression through the 1950s and 1960s. In the 1970s, Japan earned the title of the second largest economic power. Japan also has developed the second largest passenger car industry in the world!

438 After the World War II, Germany was divided into two parts— the Federal Republic of Germany (FRG) in the West and the German Democratic Republic (GDR) in the East. The city of Berlin was divided by the Berlin Wall. It was built by the East German government in 1961.

Japan emerged as an economic power in the latter part of 20th century.

A GLOBAL OUTREACH

439 Some European countries such as Canada and the USA formed an organisation called North Atlantic Treaty Organisation (NATO) in 1949. Its aim was to form an alliance based on military support. This was part of the Cold War period, and the alliance was made in case of a communist aggression.

440 Six European countries—France, Belgium, Luxembourg, West Germany, Italy, and the Netherlands—came together to form the 'Common Market' for regional growth, after signing a treaty on 25 March 1957.

441 In 1989, the Berlin Wall was taken down by the people of Berlin. After a year, the official unification of East and West Germany was put into effect. Unified Germany came to be known as the Federal Republic of Germany, with its capital in Berlin.

EXPANDING WORLD

442 **In the 1950s and 1960s, Latin America started a campaign to make its economy more stable.** The governments started industrialisation programmes to increase the production of commodities. They also encouraged trade.

443 The 1950s saw the struggle for equal rights and campaigns against segregation, especially by the Blacks in the United States. Martin Luther King led a famous movement. Segregated buses were boycotted in 1955-1956.

444 John F. Kennedy was the youngest person ever to be elected as the President of the United States in 1961. He was, however, assassinated in 1963.

A GLOBAL OUTREACH

445 **In 1963, the world leaders signed a treaty to reduce nuclear tests as a way to maintain peace.** The nuclear bombs dropped on Japan during the World War II had opened everyone's eyes towards the adverse effects of war.

446 **Sputnik 1, an artificial satellite, was sent into the orbit to study Earth by the USSR in 1957.** This caused the 'Space Race' where America too stepped up its space program in order to reach space. In 1969, astronaut Neil Armstrong became the first person to walk on the moon.

447 **The year 1990 saw an increase in the television viewing audience.** Almost 100 million families in the US came to own their own TV sets. It is believed that the era of globalisation truly began at this time, when all kinds of information became available to people inside their own homes.

448 **Papua New Guinea gained independence from Australian domination in 1975.** After gaining freedom, it started developing quite rapidly. It is home to almost six million people speaking 700 languages!

EXPANDING WORLD

449

The 20th century saw immense economic growth and changes. However, it also brought about major problems such as increased pollution and depleting natural resources.

450

Mumbai's slum area is a typical example of overpopulation. People migrate from villages to cities in search of a better life. However, the lack of accommodation and clean water in the city makes life miserable for these people. This is somewhat comparable to the situation in early industrial England, when farming communities had moved to the cities to work in factories, and had to live in cramped slums.

451

Somalia in East Africa is an example of desertification due to deforestation. Over many years, farmers cleared the land to grow crops. However, the soil was soon exhausted, resulting in desertification.

Important Personalities

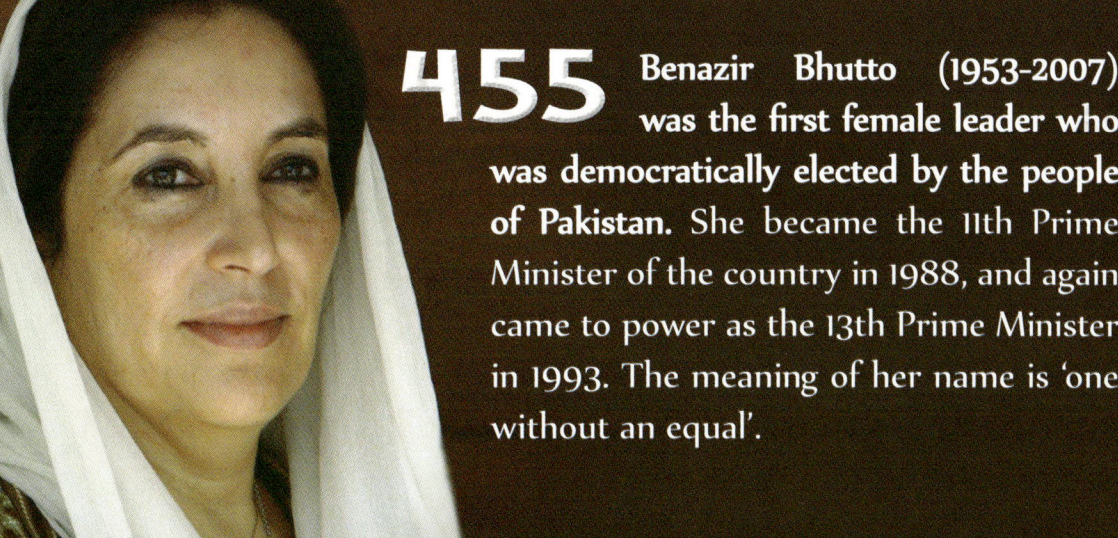

455 Benazir Bhutto (1953-2007) was the first female leader who was democratically elected by the people of Pakistan. She became the 11th Prime Minister of the country in 1988, and again came to power as the 13th Prime Minister in 1993. The meaning of her name is 'one without an equal'.

456 Sultan Raziya (1205-1240 CE) was the only female Sultan of the Delhi Sultanate. She was the daughter of Sultan Iltutmish, and came to power in 1236.

457 Maria Corazon 'Cory' Sumulong Cojuangco-Aquino (1933-2009), commonly known as Cory Aquino, became the 11th President and the first woman President of the Philippines in 1986.

452 **The Brazilian government started a project in the 1970s to build a grand North-South and East-West highway, known as the Trans-Amazonian highway.** For this, large areas of forests were cleared. It was hoped that opening this road would lead to opening up advantages of development to the poor areas of the country. However, the project failed and has been described as an ecological disaster.

453 **Did you know that since the year 1945, almost half of the rainforests of the world have been destroyed?** Deforestation leads to loss of plant and animal species.

454 **Right now, almost 90 per cent of the world's energy is derived from fossil fuels.** They cause pollution and cause environmental damage. Besides, they take millions of years to form, so once they are exhausted, it will be nearly impossible to generate more fuels. Governments around the world are now encouraging use of renewable power sources, such as solar and tidal energy.

EXPANDING WORLD

461 Nancy Grace Augusta Wake was a British Special Operations Executive agent during the World War II. The German secret service, the Gestapo, called her 'The White Mouse' because she would always manage to slip away from the German sentry's clutches.

462

Mark Twain was born in 1835. Though he is known by his pen name, his real name was Samuel Langhorne Clemens. A brilliant American author, he is famous for his classic novels 'Adventures of Tom Sawyer', and 'Adventures of Huckleberry Finn.'

IMPORTANT PERSONALITIES

458 **Mohandas Karamchand Gandhi (1869-1948) was one of the most important leaders of the Indian freedom movement.** He advocated the use of non-violent protest and has inspired generations of people across the world. He was a trained barrister, and first developed his ideas of Satyagraha, a Hindi word which when translated means 'insistence on truth', in South Africa. He joined the Indian freedom movement on his return to India in 1915. He was popularly known as 'Mahatma Gandhi' and was given the title of the 'Father of the Nation'.

459 **Neville Thomas Bonner AO (1922-1999) was the first aboriginal person to become a member of the Australian Parliament.** He became an MP in 1971 and was named Australian of the Year in 1979.

460 **Dame Nellie Melba GBE (1861-1931) was an opera singer who was famous worldwide.** She was the first Australian to gain international acclaim as a classical singer. She was born as Helen Porter Mitchell, but took on the name 'Melba' from her hometown of Melbourne.

IMPORTANT PERSONALITIES

463 Abraham Lincoln (1809-1865) was the 16th president of the United States. He belonged to a poverty stricken household and was a self-taught individual. He is well known for abolishing slavery, helping America fight through a period of civil war, which led to the unification of the Northern and Southern states.

464 Howard Walter Florey was an Australian pharmacologist and pathologist, who was involved in the development of the medicine 'penicillin'. He was awarded the Nobel Prize in Physiology/Medicine in 1945 for his life saving discovery, along with Alexander Fleming and Ernst Chain.

465 Leo Tolstoy (1828-1910) is considered one of the most influential Russian thinkers and writers of modern times. Some of his most famous novels include *War and Peace* and *Anna Karenina*. Mahatma Gandhi was deeply influenced by his ideas and named his collective farm in South Africa 'Tolstoy Farm' in 1910.

466 Billie Holiday (1915-1959) was a very famous singer. Her real name was Eleanora Fagan. She is known for changing the scene of American pop vocals forever. She had a lasting effect on jazz music.

EXPANDING WORLD

467 Simon Bolivar was born in Venezuela in 1783 and was a leader of the Latin American Revolution in South America. He was known as the 'El Libertador'.

468 Jose De San Martin was born in Argentina in the year 1778. He was known as the 'Knight of the Andes', a title given to him by the people of Argentina. He was actively involved in liberating Argentina from the Spanish Empire.

469 Gabriel García Márquez (1927-2014), the winner of the 1982 Nobel Prize for Literature, is a famous writer. He is well known for his employment of 'magical realism' into literature. Some of his most renowned books are *One Hundred Years of Solitude* and *Love in the Time of Cholera*.

IMPORTANT PERSONALITIES

470 Rigoberta Menchú Tum (born in 1959) is a political activist from Guatemala. Her aim has been to publicise the rights of Guatemala's indigenous women during and after the Guatemalan Civil War.

471 Salvador Domingo Felipe Jacinto Dalí i Domènech, the Marqués de Dalí de Pubol (1904–1989) is better known in the art world as Salvador Dalí. He was one of the most important surrealist painters. Born in Catalan in Spain, Dali's works were highly imaginative, the most famous being the oil painting 'The Persistence of Memory'.

472 Karl Marx was a philosopher, historian, revolutionary, and social scientist. He was born in Prussia in the year 1818. His works include *The Communist Manifesto* and *Das Kapital*.

EXPANDING WORLD

473

Mother Teresa (1910-1997) is the founder of the Order of the Missionaries of Charity. She dedicated her life to help the poor. In 2016, she was declared a saint by Pope Francis at the Vatican.

474
Margaret Thatcher was the Prime Minister of the United Kingdom from 1979 to 1990. She was known as the 'Iron Lady'. She was the first woman Prime Minister of England.

475
Bishop Desmond Tutu (born 1931) won the Noble Peace Prize in 1984. He fought against apartheid and for equal rights for everyone. He was the first black Archbishop of Cape Town, South Africa. He was also awarded the Nobel Peace Prize in 1984.

IMPORTANT PERSONALITIES

476 **Kofi Annan served as the seventh Secretary-General of the United Nations, from 1997 to 2006.** In 2001, he received the Nobel Peace Prize for his efforts.

477 **Cassius Clay (1942-2016) was better known to the world as Muhammad Ali.** He was a world-famous professional boxer. He also won the Olympic gold medal in 1960. He converted to Islam soon after.

478 **The Big-Bang Club was a group that emerged in South Africa between 1990 and 1994.** It included four photographers, Kevin Carter, Greg Marinovich, Ken Oosterbroek and Joao Silva. They used photography as a medium to raise awareness about apartheid.

EXPANDING WORLD

479 Wilbur and Orville Wright, better known as the Wright Brothers were pioneers in building and testing the first aircraft. The American brothers undertook their first flight on 17 December 1903, near Kitty Hawk in North Carolina.

IMPORTANT PERSONALITIES

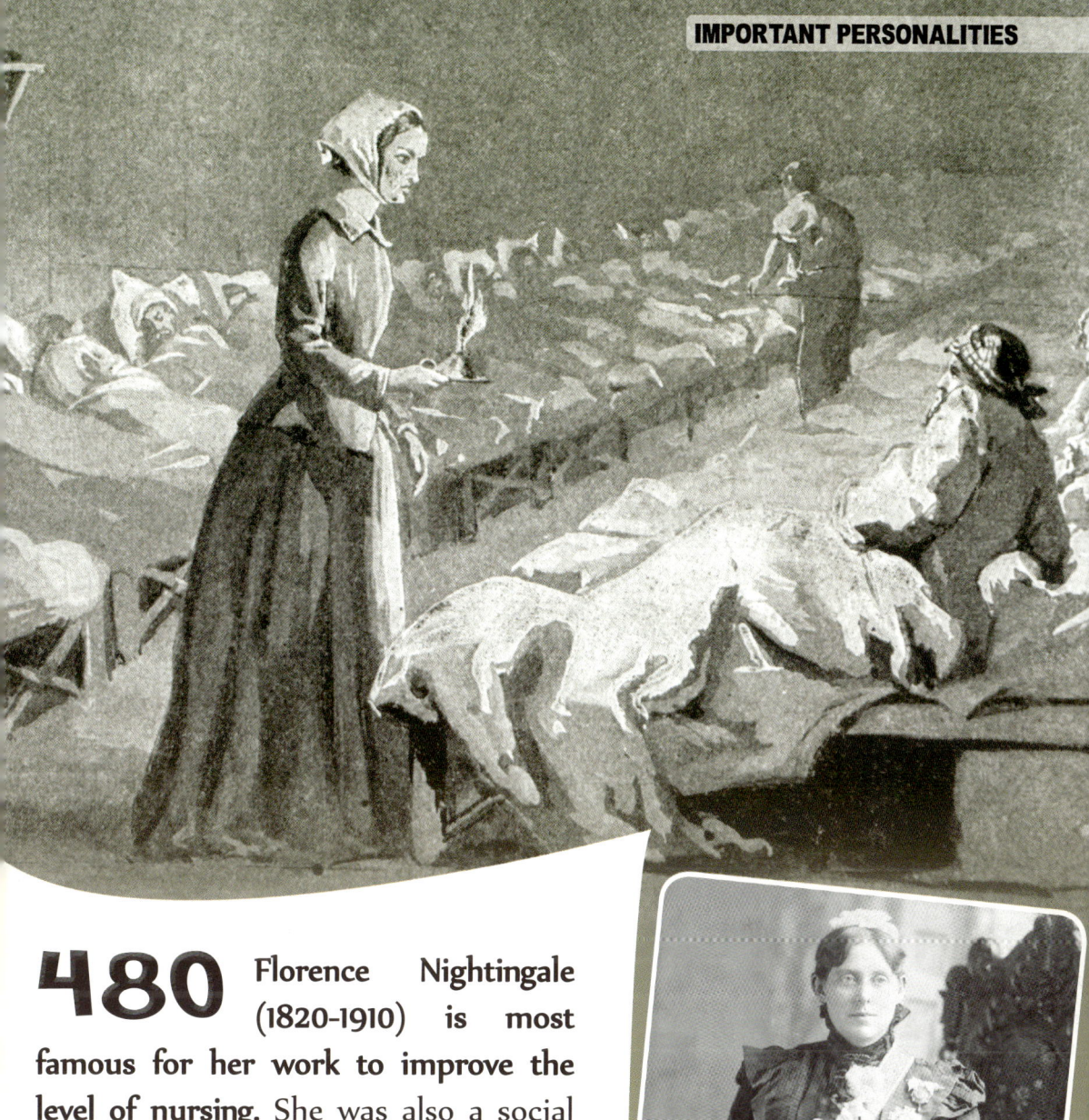

480 Florence Nightingale (1820-1910) is most famous for her work to improve the level of nursing. She was also a social reformer and came to be called the 'Lady with the Lamp'. During the Crimean War (1854) she trained and led a band of nurses to provide care and medical aid to wounded soldiers. She was also a gifted statistician and often used innovative graphic methods of representing data.

The World Today

481 **Can you imagine the sky inside your bedroom?** The Dutch visual artist Berndnaut Smilde has made it a reality! He made clouds inside closed rooms. He uses smoke and water vapour among other things to make this. His series is called 'Nimbus' and are very popular.

482 **Facebook was created in a dorm room of Harvard University by its creator Mark Zuckerberg in 2004.** Did you know that the first user to register on Facebook was not Mark, but a bot that he had created? It was not even a living being!

483 **With time many electronic devices become old and obsolete.** Have you seen a vinyl record? It was used to play music before it was replaced by cassettes. Gradually, CDs took over from cassettes and finally iPods were introduced which made CDs less popular.

THE WORLD TODAY

484 **We all know how to operate a computer.** We use the keyboard to type on the screen. However, recently a virtual keyboard has been designed, that is actually a laser projection!

485 **In 2004, Let's Corporation, a Japanese organisation introduced a project called 'Flower Sound'.** They invented a vase which hooks up to a CD player. The sound is transmitted through the flower stem and out via the petals.

486 **Humans have been observing space for years.** Newer and better devices such as telescopes have been devised for this purpose. In 2018, the most advanced telescope is supposed to be launched. NASA is building the James Webb Space Telescope, and it will be a hundred times more powerful than the present day Hubble Telescope. The JWST will be launched into outer space, from where it will transmit clear pictures of the universe back to the Earth.

EXPANDING WORLD

487 **The Tower Infinity in South Korea is also known as the invisible tower.** Estimated to be completed in 2016, the tower will allow people to see the sky right through it for a few hours every day. It is considered to be an architectural marvel.

488 **Have you heard about Google Glasses?** They let you access whatever you want right in front of your eyes, literally! They are a pair of smart glasses designed to display information in a hands-free format.

489 **Did you know it was possible to plant false memories into the mind of a living creature?** A collaborative initiative between Japanese Riken Brain Science Institute and MIT's Picower Institute for Learning and Memory has made it possible to plant artificial memory inside a mouse's brain! It is a huge breakthrough for the medical world.

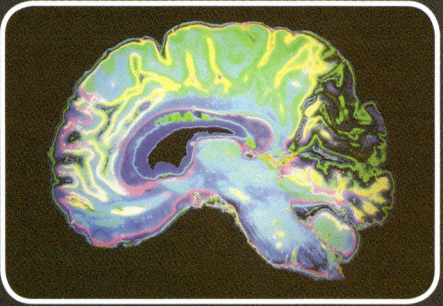

THE WORLD TODAY

490 Do you like reading books? For centuries, books have been written and printed on paper. Nowadays, books are scanned and transmitted electronically. We can read these on e-readers.

491 The internet is the greatest invention of modern times. It connects people all over the world through a wireless network. We can access information or connect with people no matter where we are.

492 Have you seen movies where the characters teleport themselves from one place to another in a jiffy? This ability may soon become reality because the researchers at Caltech are working on studying the properties of matter. If it is possible to move protons and electrons, then over time, we may be able to move larger objects as well.

EXPANDING WORLD

493 Scientists created the prototype for bionic lenses in the year 2013. These lenses can be surgically inserted into a person's eyes to restore eyesight.

494 The camera pill is a device used for medical purposes. It is small pill which has a microscopic camera inside it. It is used to detect ulcers and other diseases after a patient ingests it. Another miniature camera is used to help doctors while conducting surgeries. This is known as an endoscopy.

495 Science is progressing very quickly. We have several equipment and devices today that have improved the quality of life. One such invention is the bioartificial liver device. It can replace liver functions till a new liver is found for the patient.

496 The University of Engineering and Technology of Peru (UTEC) in collaboration with the ad agency Mayo Draft FCB have created a billboard which converts Lima's thin air into drinkable water! This could be a boon for dry and desert areas.

THE WORLD TODAY

497 The Bluetooth technology was first devised in 1999, but it only started being widely used in the 21st century. It was named after the 10th century Viking King Harald Bluetooth, who united the Danish tribes into a single kingdom. This technology is an integral part of our smartphones and other devices today.

498 One of the most important technologies today allows us to talk to each other anywhere in the world, not only through voice but also through video calling. One such technology is Skype. It was founded by the Swede Niklas Zennstrmom (Niklas Zennström) and Dane Janus Friis (Janus Friis).

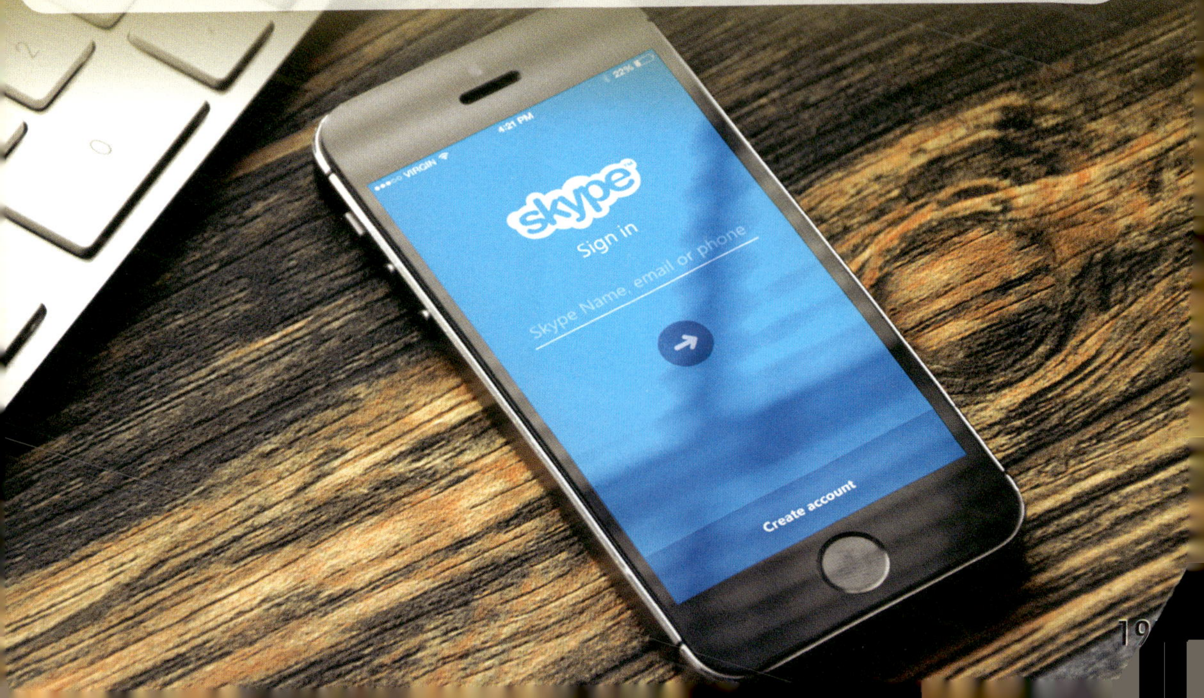

EXPANDING WORLD

499
4G has made surfing fast and less time-consuming. The fourth generation (4G) standard provides a higher mobile broadband speed. Information of the world is now available at our fingertips much easier and faster.

500
The major concern of people around the world today is ecological conservation. It is believed that if we do not take steps to protect the environment, the climate of the Earth could once again change as drastically as it did during the ice ages, millions of years ago.